Chinese Wushu S

Advanced Routines of Long-Style Boxing

Cheng Huikun

FOREIGN LANGUAGES PRESS   BEIJING

First Edition   1996

ISBN 7-119-01791-8

© Foreign Languages Press, Beijing, China, 1996

Published by Foreign Languages Press
24 Baiwanzhuang Road, Beijing 100037, China

Printed by Beijing Foreign Languages Printing House
19 Chegongzhuang Xilu, Beijing 100044, China

Distributed by China International Book Trading
Corporation
35 Chegongzhuang Xilu, Beijing 100044, China
P.O. Box 399, Beijing, China

Printed in the People's Republic of China

Contents

Contents

I. How to Learn and Practice

The advanced routines of Long-style Boxing (Chang Quan) are Wushu routines composed of the training methods for the basic skills of Chang Quan and its basic techniques. They fully reflect the style and characteristics of Chang Quan. The movements included in the advanced routines are similar to those used in the basic routine with some modifications, a large range of movement, forcefulness and graceful form. They include three hand forms, five stances, fourteen hand techniques, four foot movements, four leg techniques, three balances, four jumping movements and one tumbling movement. The playing of these routines was awarded a gold medal at the Chinese National Wushu Tournament. They call for clear distinction between motion and stillness, between quick and slow movements, with clear performances, imposing manner, and a strong sense of rhythm.

Three stages. The first stage: roughly grasp the single movements and the set combinations in the routines, make clear the line and direction of each movement, and get to know and understand the rules and timings for mutual cooperation between the upper and lower limbs and the different parts of the body. The second stage: when you practise the single movements skillfully, connect all the movements in the same routine naturally and reasonably with smooth application of power. The third stage: understand through analysis the nature, purpose, function and technical implications of the different methods of doing the exercises. Nimbly apply the skills so that the power application, rhythm of movement, the mind, the hand, eye and body techniques, as well as the footwork, are well-coordinated and the whole play is strong, brisk, hard, soft and free.

The skills in playing the Chang Quan routines are embodied in many aspects. Attention should be paid to the following points:

1. Practice the basic skills and basic movements more often to constantly improve the pliability, speed, endurance and other physical qualities. At the same time, put stress on the peculiar body techniques for Chang Quan. In the course of practice, keep in mind that the "waist is the dominant factor" and that the body should move like the crawling snake with curves and changes; the movements include closing, opening, twists, turns and inclining. For example, in Exercise 37 Press Palm with Body Turn (Figs. 3-93, 3-94, 3-95), while swinging the right arm downward, keep the chest in, withdraw the abdomen and relax the hips. Then twist the waist, turn the hips, extend the shoulders, stretch the arms and swing them separately. The forceful movement of opening and closing is mainly embodied in the twisting, folding and turning of the waist. Relax when it is closed, and accelerate when it is opened. The movement of the waist and body is vigorous and natural. Only when it is well-coordinated with the movement of the upper and lower limbs, can the movements be fully extended, flexible and smooth.

2. Gradually understand the requirement for the smooth application of power.

There must be a process of releasing power in the Wushu movements, or the movements will be drifty and loose. However, if power is not properly released, the movements will be stiff and rigid. The correct release of power is one of the basic skills embodied in the practical and demonstrative character of the Chinese Wushu. Generally speaking, the release of power from the upper limbs should be "starting at the tip, following at the middle section and accelerated at the root." The tip here denotes the hand, the middle section the elbow, and the root the shoulder. This is true for the punch, snap palm and wrist shake. Secondly, in releasing power from the upper limbs, the shoulders should be relaxed and shrugging avoided. Drop the elbow and avoid turning the elbow up when exerting the force. In releasing power from the lower limbs, it should "start at the root, pass along the middle and arrive at the tip." The root here denotes the hips, the middle section the knees and the tip the foot. This is true for the snap kick, heel kick, and side sole kick. In executing the movements of the upper and lower limbs simultaneously, in the Bow Step and Punch, for example, the power released from the feet, knees and hips must be sent to the fists through the shoulders and elbows with the waist power as the medium, so that the movements of the six joints of the upper and lower limbs are organically connected.

3. The rhythms of Chang Quan movements are one of the main criteria for the quality of the play of Chang Quan. They are the reflection of the practitioners' control ability and the depth of their understanding of the routines. In handling the rhythms of the movements, stress should be laid on the relationship between quick and slow, high and low, motion and stillness, and hard and soft. In executing the movements, these opposites transform themselves into each other. They are unified into one and should not be regarded as two separate processes.

Quick and Slow denote the change of the speed of the movement. In executing the Chang Quan routines, the speed includes two aspects: one is the duration of the time needed for completing a single movement; the other is the duration of time needed for the connection between two single movements. The total time added is the time needed for execution of the whole routine. Apart from the movement of the feet, it also includes the movements of the hand (push palm, punch and arm swinging), the upper part of the body (bending forward, bending backward, and moving to the left or right), the head, and the eyes.

In executing the whole routines, the proper handling of the rhythm changes produces the feeling of liveliness and brightness. It can embody the inherent structure of the boxing, and properly display the style and romantic charm of the sport. If the movement is quick from start to finish and fails to stop in the fixed form, it will be executed in a rush and not properly as required. Even in handling the rhythm of the single movement, there should also be change between quick and slow. In Exercise 42 "Hacking Fist With Front Toe Step", for example, the rhythm should be handled like this: turn the body to the left, relax the hips, drop the shoulders, swing the right arm forward down, then rise suddenly and change the speed from slow to quick. Hack quickly with the right fist from above downward, so that the whole movement is forceful, clear and powerful. If the movement is very quick from the very start, the range of movement will be small, the method unclear and the power insufficient.

High and Low denote the shift of the body weight. In Chang Quan, the range of rise and fall of the body weight is big and the scope of the body movement is broad. Therefore, to grasp the rule of change from high to low or vice versa helps to give full play to their technical characteristics. Jumping Lotus Kick connecting Elbow Hook with Bow Step, Jumping Front Kick connecting Hook Hand and Slap Palm with Feet Together, and Whirlwind Kick connecting Leg Splits—these are all typical exercises for High and Low. When the exercise Threading Palm with Raised Knee is connected by the exercise Threading Palm with Crouch Step, there appear rises and falls, and changes from high to low or low to high. The inclusion of these movements in the routines provides thrills to the audience and, at the same time, underlines the rhythm of the routines.

Motion and Stillness exist as two opposites. When there is motion, it runs throughout; When it is still, stillness prevails all over, as if there is a sense of firmness and stability as when thousands of horses are galloping. This is what we call, "There must be rhythm in the motion," or "There is stillness in motion." When in stillness, you must stand like a tall mountain which no powerful force can move. This is what is called, "There must be an imposing manner when in stillness." The speed varies from the single movements and combinations to parts; therefore, the methods of presenting "motion and stillness" are different. Generally speaking, they start slowly, then accelerate, and finally stop suddenly. There are also cases in which the movements both start and finish suddenly. In the slow start, the body techniques and power must be demonstrated; while in quick motion and sudden finish, the movements must be forceful and natural. Without a slow start, there is no acceleration. Without a firm stop, there is no quick movement. In exercises 19-23, the final finish for the quick punches closely followed by hook hand and snap palm with body turn and bow step must be neat and clear-cut so as to show the speed and power of the punches. In the Slap Lotus Kick, the rise and step forward must be slow, but the kick must be quick so as to show the clear difference in rhythm.

Hardness and Softness mainly show the force of the movements. Without softness for contrast, it is impossible to show the power of the hardness. "Softness" denotes the activity of the joints and pliability of the muscles, while "hardness" denotes the display of strong power. In practising boxing, force should be exerted and power released, or the movement will be powerless and loose. However, if there is only hardness but no softness, it is impossible to demonstrate all the hand, body and leg techniques of Chang Quan accurately and reasonably. When moving the left foot forward in the sweeping inside punch, for example, relax the body and make it soft, and turn it slowly and slightly to the right. Relax the right arm naturally and swing it downward, and then sweep the right fist forward and upward quickly and powerfully. Moreover, hardness and softness are also needed for the reasonable distribution of physical strength and tactical thought of Chinese Wushu. Only when hardness and softness are combined is it possible for the complete routine to rise and fall like waves, and to produce the strong rhythm of good coordination.

4. Pay attention to attack and defence.

There is a great variety of Chinese boxing. Although they form different schools and styles as a result of different attack and defence techniques, all boxing routines are based on attacking and defence movements. They take attack and defence techniques as the nucleus, and attack and defence awareness as the soul. The Wushu routines are composed of combat skills that originate from practice. Therefore, when learning the routines, you have to learn to understand the attack and defence implications and purpose of every movement after learning the movements. When the nature and true meaning of the movements are grasped, the movements will be true to their original. Now I would like to illustrate my point with a few common exercises:

(1) **Stamp Foot with Hammer Drive:** Stamping has two purposes: first, to help release power for the hammer drive, and second, to stamp on the instep of the forward-moving foot of the opponent. Hammer drive uses the back of the fist to hammer down from above, and is a defensive exercise using hardness to deal with hardness. When the opponent uses his fist or foot to attack you in the middle, you can use your fist's back to hammer the opponent's attacking fist or foot. If you practise by yourself, you can use the other palm to receive your hammering fist. (2) **Press Palm and Punch with Bow Step:** When the opponent uses his right fist to attack you, you move the left foot forward for an empty step. At the same time turn the left arm inward, elbow slightly bent, to press the left palm down on the opponent's wrist. Then straighten the right leg, bend the left leg and use the right fist to hit back at the chest or abdomen of the opponent. (3) **Raised Knee:** This has the dual purpose of attack and defence. When the opponent uses his fists to strike at your head from both sides (called "Strike Ears from Both Sides"), you step forward and move both arms upward to block the attacking forearms of the opponent. At the same time, bend your right leg and raise the knee to hit the lower part of his abdomen. This is used for attack. Another example: When you bend the left leg forward and arc your right palm forward, if the opponent uses his right arm to block it away and his right foot to hook your left shank, you raise your left leg upward quickly to block his attacking foot. At the same time turn the body slightly to the left and use the outer side of the left palm to push the opponent's chest or face. This is used for defence. (4) **Slap Kick:** Slap kick is a movement in which one palm is used to slap the instep of the kicking foot. In actual combat, both hand and foot are employed for this method. In other words, use the

palm to hit the opponent's face and use the kicking foot to hit the opponent's chest or abdomen.

Apart from that described above, the footwork, including advance, retreat and jump; the body techniques, including dodging and turning, and the slow and quick rhythms all contain the strong implications of attack and defence. They are the quintessence of the attack and defensive skills used in actual combat for a long time. If you practise as required by attack and defence, you will acquire the peculiar style of Chang Quan and at the same time improve your health and physique.

5. The movements of hand, eye, body and foot should be well-coordinated.

The Wushu exercises are exercises in which all parts of the whole body move harmoniously. The hands, eyes, body and feet all move according to their own rules, and therefore their movements should be well-coordinated. An old saying goes: "There are methods for motion, and pattern for stillness." The "methods" here refer to the methods for completing the movements through coordination among the hands, eyes, body and feet. The "pattern" refers to the finished pattern of the movement in stillness. Here I would like to stress the use of the eye techniques in the routines. The eye techniques are embodied through the movement of the head and eyes. Generally speaking, the eyes follow the movement of the hands, and the eyes cooperate with the hands. For example, in the Exercise Swing Palm with Forward Step and Thread Palm Forward, the eyes look at the right hand. When the body stands erect, move the right leg quickly forward with heel on the ground. When the chest is thrust forward and the head is bent backward, the eyes follow the movement of the left palm and then watch the right palm threaded forward. My description is long and detailed, but the movement is completed in an instant.

The turning of the head and the movement of the following eyes should be swift and bright. Moreover, coordinate with the eyes according to the movements for the attack and defence. When attacking, you must be swift and fierce with a solemn look. When defending, your look is stern, and your mind is concentrated as if you are waiting for a chance to attack. You must be full of energy in playing the complete routines so as to fully demonstrate their style and characteristics.

6. Distribution of physical strength and coordination in breathing.

The play of the Chang Quan routines not only calls for vigour, speed, power and jumping height, but also for strong physical strength so that the whole routine can be completed without interruption. However, the distribution of physical strength is also very important in the play of the whole set of exercises. Usually, the starting form and the first part are the key portions of the whole set for demonstration of the skills. Therefore, full use should be made of physical strength at the beginning of the play; this will open the movements with clear rhythms so that the exercises are done in an imposing manner. Speed acceleration and relaxation are both stressed in the second and third parts. There can be a break for rest by using the short pauses between the movements. If attention is not paid to relaxation and the whole body is always in a state of tension, a lot of physical strength will be wasted, thus affecting the execution of the following movements. In doing the fourth part, the utmost effort should be made to keep the same speed till finished. On the other hand, the pauses should be clear and neat, not sloppy. Moreover, breathing is also very important. There are four methods: "Lift, hold up, accumulate, and sink" (explained in detail in *Basics of Long-style Boxing*). These methods vary from movement to movement. The application of these methods have to be understood on the basis of natural breathing, and grasped in the course of repeated practice. One other thing worth noting: you must not hold your breath, or even breathe just once for several movements. That will lead to short breath, dizziness or sickness. As a result, your physical strength will be reduced. In order to solve this problem, pause for one or two more seconds in the major fixed forms, and do deep breathing purposely for relaxation.

To sum up, do not be impatient for success in learning Chang Quan. It is very easy to learn the patterns and process of the movements. However, if you want to do them well and display the peculiar style of the routines, it is essential to seriously understand the requirements and essential points for the execution of every movement and exercise. Persist in constant practice until you can do them skillfully and perfectly; then you will be able to acquire the style and characteristics of the routines and a fairly high technical level.

II. Names of Advanced Routines

Part One

1. Starting Form
2. Thread Forward with Feet Together
3. Horizontal Punch with Feet Together
4. Hammer Drive with Feet Together
5. Flash Palm with Side Bow Stance
6. Swing Arm and Slap Palm
7. Flash Palm with Raised Knee
8. Push Palm with Hopping Step
9. Jumping Lotus Kick with Body Turn
10. Bend Elbow with Bow Step
11. Stamp Foot with Hammer Drive
12. Double Punch with Horse-Riding Step
13. Double Palm Push with Bow Step
14. Lotus Kick with Slap
15. Hack Fist with Raised Knee
16. Jumping Front Kick with Kick Step
17. Slap Palm with Hooked Hand
18. Jump and Swing Palm
19. Brush Hand and Punch with Bow Step
20. Left Punch with Bow Step
21. Right Punch with Bow Step
22. Hook Hand and Snap Palm with Body Turn
23. Swing Palm with Cross Kick
24. Swing Palm and Thread Forward with Forward Step
25. Swing Arms to Both Sides and Turn Waist Over
26. Hack Palm with Bow Step
27. Swing Arms and Slap Palm with Crouch Step
28. Raising Knee with Upper Punch

Part Two

29. Whirlwind Kick with Kick Step
30. Whirlwind Kick with Body Turn and Forward Step
31. Pushing Palm with Side Splits
32. Sweeping Punch with Bow Step
33. Sweeping Backward with Hands Support
34. Turning Body and Threading Palm with Crouch Step
35. Pushing Palm with Snap Kick
36. Double Palm Push with Legs Crossed
37. Turn Body, Press Palm and Punch with Bow Step
38. Cross Kick
39. Punching with Bow Step
40. Turn About Face, Push Elbow with Bow Step
41. Upper Block and Punch with Bow Step
42. Hacking Fist with Front Toe Step

Part Three

43. Butterfly with Skipping Step
44. Turn Body with Hook Hand and Slap Palm
45. Side Sole Kick
46. Inside Slap Crescent Kick
47. Pushing Palm with Hooked Hand and Bow Step
48. Pressing Palm with Body Turn and Punching with Bow Step
49. Punching with Snap Kick
50. Search-Sea Balance
51. Single Slap Kick
52. Raise Knee and Push Palm

Part Four

53. Side Flip with Skipping Step
54. Turn Body and Step Forward with Heel Kick and Punch

III. Illustrated Movements

Part One

1. Starting Form

Stand with feet together, arms straight and down, fingers of both hands together against the outer sides of the thighs. Eyes front. (Fig. 3-1)

Essentials: Stand erect, head upright, neck straight, shoulders down, chest out and abdomen in. Concentrate and breathe naturally.

2. Thread Forward with Feet Together

(1) Stand with feet together, swing the arms upward to both sides, not higher than the hip level. At the same time, turn the arms inward, thumb and forefinger down, and then swing the arms downward, palms crossed facing inward in front of the abdomen, left palm outside. Then continue to swing the arms upward to above the head, elbows slightly bent. Raise the head and look at the palms. (Fig. 3-2)

(2) Swing the palms downward on both sides, then bend the elbows and withdraw them to the sides of the waist with palms obliquely up and elbow joints backward. Bend the head with the eyes on the right palm. (Fig. 3-3)

(3) Thread both palms forward simultaneously, palms facing up, and stretch the arms to shoulder level. Look ahead. (Fig. 3-4)

Essentials: The movements of swinging the arms must be connected, and the arms must be swung slowly and to the largest extent possible. While threading forward the palms,

14

Fig. 3-1   Fig. 3-2

the elbows must be placed closely by the sides of the waist to release power forward, with the power on the fingertips. Drop the shoulders, and keep the chest out and the abdomen in. Do not pause after the movement.

3. Horizontal Punch with Feet Together

(1) Turn the body to the right, right leg slightly bent, and move the left foot obliquely backward, leg straight. Swing the arms downward and past the abdomen, and then upward from both sides, both arms straight, thumbs and forefingers up, the right arm slightly higher than the left arm, and the upper part of the body slightly forward. Look at the right palm. (Fig. 3-5)

(2) Shift the body weight to the right, stand on the left leg, and move the right foot swiftly to the left foot. At the same time, change the right palm into fist, swing it forward for a horizontal punch, and arch it obliquely in front

15

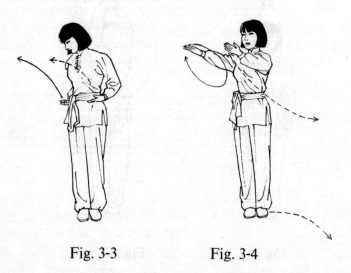

Fig. 3-3   Fig. 3-4

to the right. Change the left palm into fist, turn the arm inward and swing it downward to the left of the body, both elbows slightly bent. Immediately turn the head to the left and look left. (Fig. 3-6)

Essentials: In the process of doing exercises as described in Fig. 3-5, bend the arms first before swinging them straight upward to the right while swinging them downward. The bending and straightening of the arms should be natural and not too fast. In Fig. 3-6, the movements must be quick and clear-cut. While finishing the movements, they must be steady, and the turning of the head and the placing of feet together must be completed at the same time. Keep both shoulders down and relaxed, the chest out and the abdomen in.

4. Hammer Drive with Feet Together

(1) Turn the body slightly to the right, bend the

Fig. 3-5   Fig. 3-6

right leg to a half squat, move the left foot backward and straighten the leg, front sole on the ground. At the same time, bend the right arm and withdraw the right fist by the waist, palm facing up. Change the left fist into palm and swing it downward and forward with the upper part of the body slightly forward. Look at the left palm. (Fig. 3-7)

(2) Turn the body to the left, shift the body weight to the left leg; stand on it, bend the right leg and raise it quickly upward after stamping the ground forcefully. Place the right leg against the inner side of the left leg, instep flat. At the same time, continue to swing the left arm upward and downward to the left hip, and bend the wrist to turn the palm down. Straighten the right arm, swing it downward, past the right side of the body and raise it above the head. Look ahead obliquely to the left. (Fig. 3-8)

17

(3) Bend the left leg to half squat, drop the right leg by the inner side of the left leg, and stamp the whole right foot by the inner side of the left foot. At the same time, turn the left arm outward, bend the elbow and withdraw it to the front of the chest, palm facing up. Bend the right elbow and drop the fist in front of the body to slap the left palm with its back. Look ahead. (Fig. 3-9)

Essentials: In swinging the left arm, keep the arm straight and swing it to a large extent and at a quick speed. In stamping the right foot, the whole foot should be on the ground, producing a cracking sound simultaneously with the hammering of the fist. In bending the legs to half squat, keep the knees together and the chest out, drop the waist and avoid bending the upper part of the body forward too much and protruding the buttocks.

5. Flash Palm with Side Bow Stance

(1) Shift the body weight to the left, move the left foot one step to the left, bend the leg to half squat, and straighten the right leg to form a Side Bow Step. Swing the left arm downward and to the left. Change the right fist into palm and swing it from below to the right side. Keep both arms straight and lean the upper part of the body slightly to the left. Look at the left palm. (Fig. 3-10)

(2) Continue to swing the left arm upward to the left. Flash the left palm obliquely above the head and lower the right wrist with palm and fingers up to the right side. At the same time, turn the head to the right. Look ahead over the right palm. (Fig. 3-11)

Essentials: The difference between the Side Bow Stance and the Bow Step is to open the hips and keep the tiptoes of both feet forward. Keep the hips down and relaxed. Flashing the palms should be kept in harmony with the turning of the head. Keep the palms slightly outward. The

Fig. 3-7

ments of the arm. The head must follow the arm (Fig. 3-5, 3-6, 3-7).

2. Swing Arm and Slant Palm

(1) Turn the upper part of the body and arm to the left. Swing the right arm downward and forward, and straighten up, while the left arm is lowered to the side of the body, and is drawn backward. Draw the attention forward. Keep the weight fully on and look to the right.

(2) Turn the body to the right by making a semicircular movement, bend the right leg to the knee and straighten the left leg, while shifting the body weight. At the same time, swing the right arm upward and forward, and lower the left arm downward and to the side. Keep both arms straight and look at the right palm (Fig. 3-8).

(3) Continue to support on the body weight slightly.

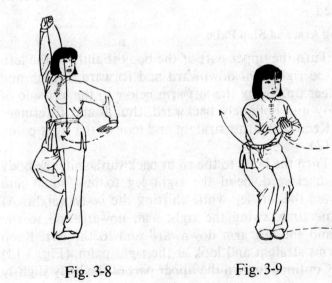

Fig. 3-8

Fig. 3-9

19

Fig. 3-10   Fig. 3-11

movements of the upper part of the body should be fully extended.

6. Swing Arm and Slap Palm

(1) Turn the upper part of the body slightly to the left, swing the right arm downward and forward, thumb and forefinger up. Swing the left arm below to the left side of the body and obliquely backward, thumb and forefinger down. Keep both arms straight and look at the right palm. (Fig.3-12)

(2) Turn the body to the right backward, shift the body weight backward, bend the right leg to half squat and straighten the left leg while shifting the body weight. At the same time, swing the right arm upward and to the right, and the left arm downward and to the left. Keep both arms straight and look at the right palm. (Fig. 3-13)

(3) Continue to turn the upper part of the body slightly

Fig. 3-12   Fig. 3-13

to the right, left heel slightly raised. Swing the left arm upward and forward, and the right arm downward and backward. Keep both arms straight while swinging them, and extend the left shoulder forward. Look at the left palm. (Fig. 3-14)

(4) Turn the upper part of the body slightly to the left, and swing the left arm down to the left, and the right arm up to the right. Keep both arms straight, the thumbs and forefingers up. Look at the right palm. (Fig. 3-15)

(5) Turn the body to the left, shift the body weight immediately forward, bend the left leg slightly, straighten the right leg and raise the heel. Swing the left palm forward, palm facing down, and continue to swing the right arm downward, forward and then obliquely upward to slap the left palm with the back. Keep both elbows slightly bent and the upper part of the body leaning forward. Look ahead. (Figs. 3-16A, B)

Fig. 3-14   Fig. 3-15

Fig. 3-16A   Fig. 3-16B

to the right left neck, slightly raise swing the left arm inward and forward, and the right arm downward and backward. Keep both arms straight while widening stance and bend the left shoulder forward. Look at the left palm (Fig. 3-14).

Turn the upper part of the body slightly to the left and swing the left arm downward and the right arm up to the right. Keep both arms straight. Thumbs and ... look at the right hand (Fig. 3-15).

... body to the left, shift the ... wards ... minute ... ly and bend the left leg, ... the ... weight ... ... The leg touches the floor, ... with ... palm forward palm facing down, and continue until the right arm downward forward and then obliquely toward to side the left palm with the back. Keep both elbows slightly bent and the upper part of the body leaning forward. Look at the right ... Figs. 3-16A, ...

Essentials: turn the waist nimbly, extend the shoulders, keep the arms straight and close to the body so as to form a vertical circle while swinging the arms. The whole process of swing the arms should be quick and continuous. Do not pause too long after finishing Fig. 3-36, but continue to do the following movement after immediately slapping the palm.

7. Flash Palm with Raised Knee

(1) Continue from the previous exercise. Move the right foot obliquely forward, leg slightly bent. Straighten the left leg forward, heel raised, and shift the body weight forward. Swing both palms downward to the abdomen and then swing the right palm obliquely upward in front of the body and the left palm obliquely downward behind the body, both arms straight and thumbs and forefingers up. Look at the right palm. (Fig. 3-17)

(2) Shift the body weight to the right leg and stand on it, bend the left leg and raise it, instep flat. Continue to swing the right arm upward and flash the right palm obliquely above the head. Shake the left wrist to form a vertical palm simultaneously, and raise it by the left side of the body. Turn the upper part of the body to the left and turn the head to the left. Look ahead to the left. (Figs. 3-18A, B)

Essentials: Keep the right knee and back straight while raising the left knee. Swing the left leg slightly to the right, shank obliquely down and turned inward. Relax both shoulders. Shake the wrists and turn the head simultaneously. Lean the trunk slightly forward to the right while tuning it to the left, so as to connect the following exercise.

8. Push Palm with Hopping Step

(1) Shift the body weight forward to the right, put the

Fig. 3-17

Fig. 3-18A   Fig. 3-18B

24

left foot obliquely ahead of the right foot, tiptoes inward. Move the right foot immediately forward to the right, tiptoes outward, and straighten the left leg forward. At the same time, swing the right palm downward, bend the elbow and withdraw it by the right side of the waist, palm facing up. Press the left palm upward, forward and downward while turning the body, finger tips pointing to the right, palm facing down and elbow slightly bent. Look forward over the left palm. (Fig. 3-19)

(2) Press the right foot against the ground forcefully, hop and jump up, body in the air. Bend and raise the left leg while swinging and turning it to the upper right, instep flat. Push the right palm up quickly from the waist side, and swing the left palm downward obliquely. Keep both arms straight, turn the upper part of the body slightly to the left and shift the body weight forward. Turn the head to the left and look ahead to the left. (Fig. 3-20)

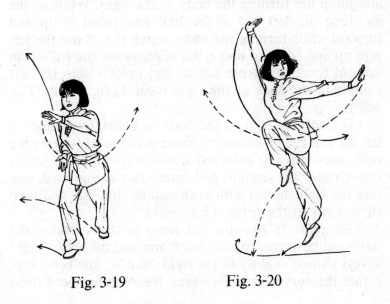

Fig. 3-19   Fig. 3-20

Essentials: The movements of stepping forward and hopping should be well-coordinated and connected, and should be immediately followed by jumping. Do not pay much attention to the jumping height, but to the shifting of the body weight forward so as to connect the following movement.

9. Jumping Lotus Kick with Body Turn

(1) Continue from the previous movement. Land the right leg naturally, move the left foot immediately and obliquely forward to the right, tiptoes slightly inward. Move the right foot obliquely forward to the right, heel on the ground and tiptoes outward, with body weight shifted slightly to the right. Swing the left arm downward, forward and upward, and the right arm close to the body from below to behind obliquely. Look ahead. (Fig. 3-21)

(2) Press the right foot against the ground forcefully and jump up, turning the body to the right. While in the air, turn the left leg to the left, and swing it up and forward while turning the body, instep flat. Raise the left arm up and forward above the head, swing the right arm upward forcefully from below, and quickly slap the left palm with the back of the right palm. Look ahead. (Fig. 3-22)

(3) Continue to turn the body to the right, swing the left leg and keep it obliquely forward to the left. Swing the right leg swiftly in a curved shape to the left and to the upper right, leg straight and instep flat and inward, and slap the right instep with both palms, first left and then right. Look at the palms. (Fig. 3-23)

Essentials: In the run and jump in this exercise, the step must be moved in a curved shape, and the body weight always shifted slightly to the right; that is, the body kept within the curved ring. However, the running speed must

Fig. 3-21

Fig. 3-22

Fig. 3-23

be quick. While jumping into the air, swing the left leg inside and keep it to the left side of the body. The right leg must be swung outward to a large extent and in the shape of a Chinese fan. The slapping should be connected, accurate and loud.

10. Bend Elbow with Bow Step

Continue to turn the body to the right while in the air, land both feet, bend the right leg to half squat, and straighten the left leg to form a bow step. Turn the upper part of the body slightly to the right. At the same time, change the left palm into fist, bend the elbow and swing the palm from left to the left chest, elbow lower than the fist. Clench the right fist and swing it to the right behind, the upper part of the body slightly forward. Look ahead. (Fig. 3-24)

Essentials: Make full use of the power released from

Fig. 3-24

turning the body to the right to form the bow step after landing, and then bend the elbow, both shoulders relaxed. The landing must be firm. Make sure that the hips are upright, relaxed and down. Avoid slating hips and protruding buttocks because of the leaning body.

11. Stamp Foot with Hammer Drive

(1) Turn the upper part of the body slightly to the right, change the left fist into palm and then swing it backward, downward and forward, thumb and forefinger facing up. Bend the right arm and withdraw the elbow by the right side of the waist, fist centre facing up. Look into the front of the left palm. (Fig. 3-25)

(2) Turn the body to the left, shift the body weight to the left leg and stand on it, heel raised. Bend the right leg and raise it up quickly after pressing it against the ground forcefully, right foot close to the inner side of the left leg, instep flat. At the same time, continue to swing the left arm upward, and then to the lower left. Press it obliquely below to the left side of the body, and swing the right arm from right upward to above the head and immediately clench the fist. Look ahead. (Fig. 3-26)

(3) Land the right foot in the inner side of the left foot, stamp the whole foot on the ground, and then bend the knee to half squat. While stamping the foot, swing the left foot upward quickly towards the back side of the right shank, instep close to the back side of the right knee, instep flat. Turn the left arm outward, bend the elbow and withdraw it to the front of the right side of the waist, palm facing up. Bend the right elbow, drop the right fist, and slap the left palm quickly with the back of the fist. Lean the upper part of the body slightly to the right, chest in. Lower the head, with eyes on the right fist. (Fig. 3-27)

Essentials: Do not pause in the movement. Although

the upper part of the body is leaned to the right while stamping the foot and squatting, the body weight should tend forward to the left. The chest should be kept in tightly and the upper part of the body should not lean forward.

12. Double Punch with Horse-Riding Step

Shift the body weight to the left, move the left foot quickly one step to the left, tiptoes forward, and bend both legs to a half squat to form the horse-riding step. Clench both fists and punch from the waist to both sides of the body, fist centres facing down, both arms straight, and the upper part of the body tilting slightly to the left side. Turn the head to the left and look ahead to the left. (Fig. 3-28)

Essentials: Shift the body weight to the left first, and then move the left foot closely to the ground to the left. To keep the body from rising and falling, it is essential to avoid standing on the right leg and bending the leg again to form the horse-riding step as a result of moving the left foot after stamping the right foot and bending the knee to half squat. In punching, relax the shoulders and stretch the arms, extend the upper part of the body fully in sharp contrast to the foot stamping and hammering the fist. Keep the chest out and drop the waist in forming the horse-riding step.

13. Double Push Palm with Bow Step

While changing the fists into palms, bend the elbows and withdraw them to the waist side. Turn the body to the left, bend the left leg to half squat and straighten the right leg to form the bow step. At the same time, push the right palm forward to the right and the left palm backward to the left, forcefully, both arms straight, palm fingers up, left palm higher than the right palm, and trunk slightly forward to the right. Look ahead at the right palm. (Fig. 3-29)

Fig. 3-25   **Fig. 3-26**

Fig. 3-27   **Fig. 3-28**

Describing a big curve, step to straighten the right leg by using the waist and pushing the slap should be completed at the same time. While straightening the right leg, attention should be paid to the coordination with the chest, hips, and the turning of the right foot outward. The palm should move quickly and reach the highest position, with the palm centre facing upward at the calf's rising time. Sole of the right foot should be raised, toes up, and the instep of the foot taut.

14. Lunge to Punch:

(1) Shift body weight to the right. Bend on the right leg, slightly raise the left foot, rise, and the right foot, meanwhile kick out again turn around (carefully in coordination with the shift of the body weight), keep front sole on the ground, set up the turn downward.

Fig. 3-29

Essentials: The movements of straightening the right leg, twisting the waist and pushing the palms should be completed at the same time. While straightening the right leg, attention should be paid to the coordination with the closed hips and the turning of the right heel outward. The palms should be pushed quickly and to the most outward position, with power applied to the outer edge of the palms. It is only a change of the step, so there should be no rise and fall in the shift of the body weight.

14. Lotus Kick with Slap

(1) Shift the body weight to the right. Stand on the right leg, quickly move the left foot obliquely behind the right foot after pressing the left foot against the ground forcefully in coordination with the shift of the body weight; keep front sole on the ground. Swing the right arm downward, past the body and upward, placing the right

palm above the head to the right. Swing the left palm forward, bend the elbow and withdraw the palm in front of the right shoulder, fingers up. Look obliquely ahead. (Fig. 3-30)

(2) Move the left foot half a step forward to the left, shift the body weight forward to the left leg, and straighten the right leg, heel raised. Swing the left arm downward and to the left, palm facing down, and the right arm downward and to the upper left. Slap the left palm with the back in front of the head, both arms slightly bent. Look at the palms. (Fig. 3-31)

(3) Stand on the left leg, and swing the right leg to the left, upward and to the right in a curved shape with a kick, instep flat and slightly inward. Move the palms upward and slap the right instep with them, first the left and then the right. Keep both legs straight and look ahead. (Fig. 3-32)

Essentials: The moving of the left foot and the swinging of the right leg should be closely connected. The swinging movement should be fan-shaped. The main point is to kick the right leg towards the left forward and then swing it to the right quickly. The slapping should be clear and loud. Keep the hips open and the knees straight.

15. Hack Fist with Raised Knee

(1) Continue to swing the right leg from right downward and land it on the right side, leg straight. At the same time, turn the body to the left and bend the left leg to half squat to form the bow step. Move the right arm, downward and forward, fist centre facing up. Move the left palm downward, bend the elbow and press it to the inner side of the right forearm, palm facing down. Look at the right fist. (Fig. 3-33)

(2) Turn the body to the right, shift the body weight to

Fig. 3-30

Fig. 3-31   Fig. 3-32

the right, and stand on the right leg. After kicking the ground, bend the left leg quickly and raise it up, instep flat. Turn the right arm inward and hack the fist to the right from above. Swing the left arm upward, and flash the palm above the head to the left. Turn the head to the right and look ahead to the right. (Fig. 3-34)

Essentials: Keep the supporting leg straight. Grip the ground with all five toes of the right foot and stand firmly. Raise the left leg as high as possible, shank obliquely down and inward. The hacking movement should be executed quickly and forcefully. Keep the arm straight and apply the power to the fist wheel. The whole exercise should be done first slowly and then quickly.

16. Jumping Front Kick with Kick Step

(1) Move the left foot to the left and shift the body weight to the left. Move the right foot immediately for-

Fig. 3-33　　　　　Fig. 3-34

ward to the left for a front cross step, tiptoes slightly outward, and shift the body weight again to the right leg, left heel raised. Change the right fist into palm, and swing it upward and to the left to chop down, fingertips forward, thumb and forefinger up. Move the left arm down at the same time, bend the elbow and withdraw the left palm to under the right forearm, palm facing down. Look ahead to the left. (Fig. 3-35)

(2) Press the left foot against the ground forcefully and jump up. Beat the left foot with the right foot quickly in the air, both legs straight. At the same time, swing the arms upward on both sides, both arms straight, thumbs and forefingers up, with body weight forward. Look ahead to the left. (Fig. 3-36)

(3) Land the right foot first and then land the left foot immediately forward to the left, tiptoes slightly outward. Turn the body slightly to the left, and move the right foot forward, heel on the ground and leg straight. At the same time, move the left arm upward and the right arm naturally down. Look ahead. (Fig. 3-37)

(4) While shifting the body weight forward, land the right foot on the ground, press the ground forcefully, jump up and swing the left leg upper forward. Bend the left arm and withdraw it over the head. Swing the right arm downward, forward and upward to slap the left palm with the back, both arms slightly bent. Look ahead. (Fig. 3-38)

(5) Bend the left leg in the air, withdraw it in front of the body, and swing the right leg quickly to the upper forward, instep flat. At the same time, drop the right palm quickly to slap the right instep, and raise the left arm to the upper left, bending the upper part of the body slightly forward. Look at the right palm. (Fig. 3-39)

Essentials: The movements of running and moving the foot forward should be quick and connected so as to

Fig. 3-35   Fig. 3-36

Fig. 3-37   Fig. 3-38   Fig. 3-39

achieve the utmost power for the jump-up. The purpose of landing the right heel on the ground first in preparing for the jump is to make efficient use of inertia to achieve the best jumping height. The slapping movement should be completed at the highest point of the jump. When slapping the right foot, make sure that the left leg is drawn back in front of the body. The slapping should be accurate and loud.

17. Slap Palm with Hooked Hand

Keep the feet together and land them at the same time, heels slightly raised, and bend the knees to full squat. While squatting, pat the ground with the right palm, swing the left arm downward, backward and upward, and change the left palm into hooked hand, hook point up. Look ahead at the ground. (Fig. 3-40)

Essentials: While patting the ground, keep the whole right palm on the ground; the movement should be quick and forceful. The power should be applied to the palm. While bending the body forward and patting the ground, keep the knees apart and the heels together and slightly raised. This helps to avoid bending the back and protruding the buttocks. There should be no pause in the movement.

18. Jump and Swing Palm

Continue from the previous movement. Press both feet against the ground and jump up. Bend the left leg, shank backward and upward to the right, and swing the right shank forward to the left, legs crossed and insteps flat. Twist the trunk forward to the right. Swing the right arm in front of the body, upward and to the right, and swing the left arm from below to the upper left, placing the palm above the head. Turn the head to the right and look ahead to the right. (Fig. 3-41)

Essentials: The reaction force from the squatting in the

Fig. 3-40   Fig. 3-41

previous exercise is used for the jump-up in this exercise. Therefore, the exercise must be closely connected with the preceding movement. Keep the chest out, extend the abdomen, and swing the left shank as far as possible. The whole movement should be executed smoothly and naturally.

19. Brush Hand and Punch with Bow Step

(1) Turn the body to the right, land the right leg first and bend it to half squat. Land the left foot backward to the left, foot entirely on the ground, and straighten the leg to form the bow step. At the same time, change the right palm into fist, bend the elbow and draw it back to the right side of the waist, fist centre up. Bend the left arm in front of the body and swing the left palm to the front of the right shoulder, fingers obliquely up. Look ahead. (Fig. 3-42)

(2) Turn the body to the left, bend the right leg to full squat, knee outward, and lay the left leg entirely on the

ground, tiptoes inward and the whole foot on the ground. Keep the trunk in the same position, but tilted slightly to the left. Look ahead to the left. (Fig. 3-43)

(3) Continue to turn the body to the left, shift the body weight forward, straighten the right leg, and bend the left leg to half squat to form the left bow step. Turn the left arm inward with the thumb pointing down. Swing the left palm from the front of the body horizontally backward to the left. After passing the outer side of the left foot, clench the fist and turn the arm outward simultaneously, drawing it back to the left side of the waist, fist centre up. At the same time, thrust the right fist horizontally forward, fist centre down. Look ahead. (Fig. 3-44)

Essentials: While landing the left foot, brush the ground with the outer side of the foot. It is not advisable to land the left foot after straightening the left leg. This is because it is not easy to keep the body firm. In brushing the left hand, move the palm quickly with the thumb and the forefinger close to the instep. In thrusting the fist, twist the waist, extend and relax the shoulders. In forming the bow step, do not keep the heel off the ground. The movements of brushing and thrusting should be coordinated and connected. The power should be applied to the fist face. Do not pause after finishing the movement.

20. Left Punch with Bow Step

Continue from the previous movement. Turn the trunk slightly to the right and thrust the left fist horizontally forward, fist centre down. Bend the right elbow and draw the fist back to the right side of the waist. Keep the bow step unchanged. Look ahead at the left fist. (Fig.3-45)

Essentials: Make use of the power from turning the body to the right for thrusting the left fist, extend the left shoulder and relax the right shoulder. Do not pause after finishing the movement.

Fig. 3-42

...

Fig. 3-43   Fig. 3-44

41

Fig. 3-45

21. Right Punch with Bow Step

Continue from the previous movement and keep the bow step unchanged. Turn the trunk to the left and thrust the right fist forward. Turn the left arm outward, bend it and draw the fist back to the left side of the waist, fist centre up. Look ahead. (Fig. 3-44)

Essentials: The exercises from 19 to 21 should be connected without interruption, quickly and forcefully. While thrusting the fist, turn the forearm inward. While drawing the fist back to the waist side, turn the arm outward in coordination with the fist thrusting. In thrusting the fist, there is no change in the height of the bow step, except for the turn of the trunk. Keep the right leg straight. Do not pause after finishing the movement.

22. Hook Hand and Snap Palm with Body Turn

(1) Continue from the previous exercise. Turn the trunk slightly to the right, change the right fist into palm,

bend the elbow and press it down, fingers to the left and palm facing down. Change the left fist into palm, palm facing up, and thrust it forward above the back of the right hand, arm straight. While thrusting the left palm above the right hand, bend the right arm and place the right palm under the left arm. Look at the left palm. (Fig. 3-46)

(2) Turn the body to the right, shift the body weight to the right, bend the right leg to half squat, and straighten the left leg, heel outward, to form the right bow step. Turn the right arm outward, back of the hand facing the body. Swing the palm downward, to the right and forward, and bend the wrist up to form a standing palm, fingers up. Change the left palm into hook, and raise it on the left side of the body. Tilt the trunk forward to the right. Turn the head to the right and look at the right palm. (Fig. 3-47)

Essentials: The swinging of the trunk must precede the movements of the lower limbs. In other words, the right

Fig. 3-46   Fig. 3-47

palm is swung downward and past the central line of the body before shifting the body weight and changing to the right bow step. Otherwise, it is difficult to coordinate the movements of the upper limbs and lower limbs. The straightening of the left leg, the turning of the heel outward and the hips should all be coordinated with the turning of the body to the right. They should be completed simultaneously with palm snapping and hand hooking. The movements should be clean and natural. No part of the body should be allowed to shake in the fixed position to show the quickness and urgency of the three consecutive thrusts.

23. Swing Palm with Cross Kick

(1) Shift the body weight to the left, and land the right foot behind the left foot, front sole on the ground and both legs bent to half squat. At the same time, swing the right palm upward and to the left shoulder, fingers up. Bend the elbow and place it close to the body. Raise the left arm on the left side, bend the trunk forward, chest close to the left thigh. Look ahead or look at the ground in front. (Fig. 3-48)

(2) Swing the right arm downward and to the right, change the left hook into palm and raise it on the left side. Keep both arms straight. Pivot on the balls of both feet and turn backward to the right, face about. Swing the right arm upward and to the right, and the left arm downward and to the left simultaneously. Look ahead to the right. (Fig. 3-49)

(3) Continue to turn the body to the right, shift the body weight forward, straighten the left leg, and move the left foot half a step forward behind the right foot, ball on the ground. At the same time, continue to swing the right arm downward and backward, and the left arm upward

and forward, both arms straight. Look at the left palm. (Fig. 3-50)

(4) Stand on the right leg, swing the left leg quickly forward and upward, instep flat and both legs straight. At the same time, continue to swing the right arm upward and forward to quickly pat the left instep with the right palm. Swing the left arm from below backward. Look at the right palm. (Fig. 3-51)

Essentials: While swinging the arms, keep them straight and close to the body. The swinging must be quick and the waist must be nimble in turning. When patting the left instep, the fingers of the right palm must point to the left to form an horizontal palm. The patting should be accurate and loud. Keep the supporting leg straight. Do not shrug the shoulders and bend the back.

24. Swing Palm and Thread Forward with Forward Step

(1) Bend the right leg slightly and move the left foot backward, ball on the ground. Move the right arm down in front of the body and swing the left palm from below to the right to the inner side of the right upper arm, fingers up. Look ahead at the right palm. (Fig. 3-52)

(2) Shift the body weight to the left, stand on the left leg, move the right leg obliquely backward to the left, and place it by the rear side of the left leg, tiptoes on the ground. At the same time, swing the arms downward, to the left and upward, and turn the trunk slightly to the left and to the right while swinging the arms. Keep the chest out and the head up. The eyes follow the swinging of the palms (first the left and then the right). (Fig. 3-53)

(3) Turn the body slightly to the right, shift the body weight forward, move the right foot forward, tiptoes outward, and straighten the left leg, heel off the ground. Continue to swing the left arm upward and forward and

| Fig. 3-48 | Fig. 3-49 |

| Fig. 3-50 | Fig. 3-51 |

press it down. Extend the left shoulder forward, arm slightly bent and palm facing down. After swinging the right palm downward, bend the elbow and withdraw the palm to the right side of the waist, palm facing up. Look at the left palm. (Fig. 3-54)

(4) Tilt the body forward, move the left foot obliquely forward, and straighten the right leg, heel off the ground. Thrust the right palm forward from above the back of the left hand, arm straight and palm facing up. Swing the left arm from below backward, automatically. Look ahead at the right palm. (Fig. 3-55)

Essentials: Relax the arms and swing the palms in a vertical circle. Keep the waist nimble in turning to increase the range of the swing. Keep the body weight forward while moving the step forward and threading the palm so as to connect the following movements. No pause after the movement,

25. Swing Arms to Both Sides and Turn Waist Over

(1) Continue from the previous movement. Move the right foot immediately obliquely forward to the right, tiptoes outward. Straighten the left leg and shift the body weight forward. Turn the right arm inward so that the palm faces down. Bend the left elbow and thrust the left palm from the waist side, and then from above the back of the right palm, and thread it forward. Bend the right arm so that the right palm is placed under the left upper arm, palm facing down. Look ahead at the left palm. (Fig. 3-56)

(2) Shift the body weight forward, press the right leg against the ground and jump up. Swing the left leg forward. While jumping up, turn the body to the right, legs apart. Swing the right arm downward and to the right, and raise the left arm on the left side, both arms straight with

Fig. 3-52   Fig. 3-53

Fig. 3-54   Fig. 3-55

thumbs up. Look ahead. (Fig. 3-57)

(3) Land the left foot to the left side of the body, tiptoes outward, and then bend the knee to half squat. Move the right foot immediately behind the left foot to the left, ball on the ground and thighs closely together. At the same time, swing the right arm upward, past the chest and to the front of the left shoulder, fingers up. Turn the left arm inward with thumb down and raise it up on the left side. Bend the trunk forward, chest close to the thigh. Look at the ground in front. (Fig. 3-58)

(4) Keep both legs to half squat. Swing the right arm downward and to the right. Keep both arms straight with thumbs down. Look at the ground in front. (Fig. 3-59)

(5) Turn the trunk over to the right and bend backward. At the same time, pivot on the balls and turn both feet, tiptoes forward and both legs straight. Swing the right arm from above and the left arm from elbow to describe a circle. Extend the abdomen, keep the chest out and bend the head backward. Look backward. (Fig. 3-60)

(6) Continue to turn the trunk over, keep the right foot in the same position, bend the right leg to half squat, straighten the left leg, left heel outward and slightly raised. Swing the left arm from above forward, and the right arm from below backward to describe a circle. Extend the left shoulder forward and keep both arms straight. Look ahead at the left palm. (Fig. 3-61)

(7) Continue to turn the trunk to the left downward. Withdraw the left heel and place the whole foot on the ground. Bend the legs to half squat and shift the body weight slightly to the right leg. Swing the left arm downward and to the left, and the right arm downward and to the right simultaneously, both arms straight. Bend the trunk forward and look obliquely down. (Fig. 3-62)

(8) Stand on the right leg. Raise the heel, pivot on the

Fig. 3-56   Fig. 3-57

Fig. 3-58   Fig. 3-59

front sole, and turn. Bend the left leg and raise it up, shank obliquely down and inward, and instep flat. At the same time, continue to turn the trunk over to the upper left and bend it backward. Swing the left arm upward and to the left, and the right arm downward and to the right simultaneously in a circle to both sides of the body, arms straight, and palms facing obliquely up. Extend the abdomen, thrust the chest forward, raise the head and bend the trunk backward. Look backward. (Fig. 3-63)

(9) Continue to turn the trunk over to the left, and swing the right arm upward and to the right, and the left arm downward and to the left simultaneously. Stand on the right leg, and continue to pivot on the right ball while turning the trunk over. Then bend the knees to full squat, and land the left foot obliquely before the right foot, tiptoes outward, keep the body weight between the legs. Look ahead to the right. (Fig. 3-64)

Essentials: In the movements described in Fig. 3-57, do not jump too high, but take a small step crosswise. While swinging the arms, make the waist nimble, extend and relax the shoulders, and keep both arms straight and close to the body to describe circles quickly. Do not rise and fall too much while turning the trunk over. After finishing the first turn-over, there should be relaxation and the speed properly reduced so that the second turning over is even quicker than the first. The whole process of turning the trunk over should be smooth and continuous, and the shift of the body weight should be natural and well-coordinated.

26. Hack Palm with Bow Step

(1) Shift the body weight forward and stand on the left leg. After stepping on the ground, bend the right leg quickly, raise it and place the right foot against the inner side of the left knee, instep flat. Raise the left arm up from

Fig. 3-60

Fig. 3-61

Fig. 3-62

Fig. 3-63

the left side and swing the right arm downward, to the left and upward in a circle to slap the left palm with the back of the right hand over the head, both arms slightly bent. Look ahead. (Fig. 3-65)

(2) Shift the body weight forward to the right, move the right foot forward to the right, bend the knee to half squat, and straighten the left leg to form the right bow step. At the same time, hack down with the right palm to the right, fingers up. Change the left palm into fist, swing it downward, bend the elbow and withdraw it to the left side of the waist, fist centre up. Lean the trunk forward to the right and turn the head to the right. Look ahead to the right palm. (Fig. 3-66)

Essentials: While hacking downward, shift the body weight first before moving the step, and step forcefully with the right foot. In Fig. 3-65, raise the right knee as high as possible and also the left heel, but slowly. In Fig. 3-66, make the bow step as soon as the right foot lands on the ground. The distance between the feet for the bow step should be well placed, as well as the height. The making of the bow step and the hacking should be completed at the same time, quickly and forcefully, so as to show different speed and height.

27. Swing Arms and Slap Palm with Crouch Stance

(1) Shift the body weight to the left, bend the left knee to half squat, and straighten the right leg. Twist the trunk to the left. At the same time, swing the right arm downward and forward, arm straight and thumb up. Change the left fist into palm and swing it upward, bend the elbow and place it by the inner side of the right upper arm. Look at the right palm. (Fig. 3-67)

(2) Shift the body weight to the right, bend the right leg to half squat, straighten the left leg and turn the trunk

the left side, and turning the right arm downward, to the left and upward in a circle to stop the left palm with the back of the right hand over the head, both arms slightly bent. Look ahead (Fig. 3-63).

(2) Shift the body weight forward to the right, move the right foot forward to the right the same, the eyes to the right, and straighten the left leg to form the right bow step. At the same time, bring downward the right palm of the right hand, and then left palm into the bow step... downward, bring the ... to the left side of the waist. Extend the ... with the right hand to (Fig. 3-65 and turn the body to the front, turn to the right ... right palm (Fig. 3-66).

Essentials: While backing toward, shift the body weight first before moving the step, and stop forcefully with the right foot. In Fig. 3-3, raise the right knee as high as possible and also ... to form... In Fig. 3-64, ... make the bow step as soon as the right foot finds on the ground. The distance between the feet of the bow step should be well placed as well as ... of the bow step and the moving step ... completed at the same time, smoothly and fast enough to match ... movement and turning.

Fig. 3-64

Fig. 3-65   Fig. 3-66

to the right. At the same time, swing the right arm upward and to the forward right, and the left arm downward and to the left, both arms straight and thumbs up. Look ahead to the right. (Fig. 3-68)

(3) Continue to turn the trunk to the right, left heel slightly raised. At the same time, swing the right arm downward and backward, and the left arm upward and forward. Twist the waist and extend the left shoulder forward. Look ahead. (Fig. 3-69)

(4) Turn the trunk to the left, shift the body weight to the left, and bend the left leg to full squat, tiptoes and knee outward, and straighten the right leg on the ground to form the crouch stance. Swing the right arm upward and downward, and pat the ground with the right palm in the inner side of the right foot while in the crouch stance. Swing the left arm from below obliquely to the left, and lean the trunk to the right side. Look ahead to the right. (Fig. 3-70)

Essentials: In the process of describing vertical circles, keep the arms close to the ears when they are moved up, and close to the legs when they are down. Make the waist nimble and extend the shoulders. The movements must be executed quickly. In shifting the body weight, do not move the left foot to and fro, but raise the heel slightly so as to ensure that the body weight is stable in swinging the arms. The patting should be close to the inner side of the foot. If the pliability is not sufficient, just slap the palm close to the inner side of the right leg. Do not bend the trunk forward nor raise the left heel. Otherwise, you will lose your balance and fall to the ground.

28. Raising Knee with Upper Punch

Bend the right leg and shift the body weight to between the legs, and then to the right leg. Straighten the right leg

Fig. 3-67

Fig. 3-68

Fig. 3-69

Fig. 3-70

forcefully and stand on it. Bend the left leg quickly and raise it up. Change the right palm into fist, bend the elbow, withdraw it to the right side of the waist, and thrust it upward from the right earside, arm straight, and fist eye backward. Swing the left palm from above obliquely forward on the right, bend the elbow quickly and withdraw it to the front of the right shoulder, fingers up and elbow lower than the hand. Lean the trunk slightly forward to the left, turn the head to the left and look ahead to the left. (Fig. 3-71)

Essentials: Turn the head while raising the knee and thrusting the fist upward. All three movements should be completed simultaneously. The force should reach the face of the fist when it is thrust upward. While standing on the right leg, the knee straight and the toes gripping the ground, and pause for two or three seconds. The raised knee is placed neither upright nor sideways, shank inward

Fig. 3-71

and instep flat. For the movement of the left arm, please refer to Fig. 3-30 or Fig. 3-43.

Part Two

29. Whirlwind Kick with Kick Step

(1) Shift the body weight to the left, move the left foot forward to the left, tiptoes outward and leg slightly bent. Immediately afterward, bend the right leg slightly, heel raised. Change the right fist into palm and press it downward and forward to the left, palm facing down, right shoulder forward and arm slightly bent. At the same time, change the left palm into fist and swing it to the lower left. Bend the elbow and withdraw the fist to the left side of the waist, fist centre up. Shift the body weight forward to the left. Look ahead to the left. (Fig. 3-72)

(2) Press the left leg against the ground forcefully and jump up. Slap the inner side of the left foot immediately with the right foot. Keep both legs straight. At the same time, push the left arm forward from above the back of the right palm to the left while changing the left fist into palm, fingers up. Turn the right arm outward, bend the elbow and withdraw the right palm to the right side of the waist, palm facing up. Shift the body weight forward to the left. Look ahead to the left. (Fig. 3-73)

(3) Land the right foot on the ground, move the left foot forward to the left. Then pivot on the ball of the left foot, turn the body to the left, and move the right foot half a step forward to the right, ball on the ground, both legs slightly bent and right knee slightly inward. Shift the body weight slightly to the right leg. At the same time, swing the right arm from above forward to the right, bend the left elbow and withdraw the left palm to the front of the

right shoulder. Bend the trunk slightly forward to the right. Look obliquely down. (Fig. 3-74)

(4) Shift the body weight to the right. When it is shifted fully to the right leg, step on the ground and jump up quickly. Bend the left leg and swing it to the upper left, and immediately turn the body to the upper left. Swing the left arm up. Swing the right arm downward to the side of the body. Look to the upper left. (Fig. 3-75)

(5) While in the air, continue to turn the body to the left. Bend the left leg and swing it upward. Swing the right leg quickly from right to upper left for an inside kick, tiptoes flexed upward. Bend the left arm to slap the ball of the right foot with the left palm, and raise the right arm naturally by the right side of the body. (Fig. 3-76)

(6) Continue to turn the body to the left in the air. Land both feet simultaneously, heels raised and knees bent for a cushioning effect. Swing the right arm from above to the right side of the body. Bend the left arm and swing it to the right shoulder. Look ahead to the right. (Fig. 3-77)

Essentials: Avoid jumping too high in the kick step so as not to affect the forward impulsive force. In starting for the jump, shift the body weight to the right leg so as to jump up to achieve the best height for the whirlwind kick. However, quite often, the body is not turned enough to the left or the body weight is not shifted forward enough in the turning because the leg power is not sufficient or the left leg is used to add power. In swinging the left leg upward, either bent leg or straight leg is permitted. In either way, the leg should be swung as high as possible so as to connect the following movement. In swinging the right leg, two points should be stressed: first, keep the leg straight and close to the body (in other words, kick up before swinging it to the left); second, swing the leg from

Fig. 3-72   Fig. 3-73

Fig. 3-74   Fig. 3-75

Fig. 3-76   Fig. 3-77

right to upper left in the shape of a Chinese fan. The slapping should be accurate and loud. If the spring is strong, land the right leg after the slapping in order to connect the following movement. Keep the ball on the ground, the knee joint slightly inward and the knee bent for a buffer, with a slight forward impulse to the right. Step, jump, arm swinging, body turning and the inside kick should be well-coordinated.

30. Whirlwind Kick with Body Turn and Forward Step

(1) Pivot on the ball of the right foot, and turn the body 180 degrees to the left. Raise the left foot, and move it to the left as soon as the body is turned to the desired position, tiptoes outward and heel off. Then pivot on the ball of the left foot and continue to turn the body 180 degrees to the left. Move the right foot half a step forward to the right, front sole on the ground, tiptoes and knee

inward, both legs slightly bent for the jump. Shift the body weight slightly to the right leg, raise the right arm while turning the body, bend the left arm and place it in front of the chest. Bend the trunk slightly forward to the right. Look obliquely down. (See Fig. 3-74)

(2) The movement is the same as described in Exercise Twenty-nine (4). (See Fig. 3-75)

(3) The movement is the same as described in Exercise Twenty-nine (5). (See Fig. 3-76)

Essentials: The points for the whirlwind kick are the same as described in Exercise Twenty-nine. The body turn and forward step must be connected, coordinated and good for the jump for the second whirlwind kick. While landing both feet and turning the body you should keep the body weight always forward, and in moving either foot forward and turning the body, keep the body weight shift natural and connected with no pause; in moving either foot forward, keep both heels off the ground, because the body turn is immediately followed by the step and jump for the whirlwind kick. If the feet land on the ground, you have to again step on the ball first, thus increasing the time, reducing the speed and causing an unnecessary pause in the execution of the movements; the left body turn should be a complete turn of 360 degrees, not a turn of two separate parts. As to when and from what angle to move the foot forward, it should be a natural movement in the process of turning the body. The guiding principles are that the movement is not awkward and power can be exerted. The forward step should be flexible and natural. Beginners should first follow the instructions and steps as described in the book. Flexibility is allowed only after you are well acquainted with the movements. If the body is turned with only one leg on the ground, keep the right foot and knee slightly inward and turn the body 180 degrees to the left, and then immediately move the left foot forward, followed by a 180-degree left turn of the body. At this stage, the left step forward with a left body turn should be closely connected with the right step forward for the jump. The forward impulsive force should be well used for the second jump. This is the difference between the single foot landing with body turn and the landing with both feet for the whirlwind kick. It requires good spring, speed and power. The left leg should have strong control ability.

31. Pushing Palm with Side Splits

Continue to turn the body to the left in the air. Turn the left tiptoes upward and swing the left foot forward. Swing the right leg down, turn the hip and straighten the leg. Land both legs on the ground to form side splits, legs straight, front foot up right and rear instep flat. Push both palms from the chest simultaneously to the two sides of the body, fingers up and arms straight. Look ahead. (Fig. 3-78)

Essentials: After the slapping in the whirlwind kick, turn the right hip and keep the right knee straight, and stretch the leg as far back as possible. In this way, the knee joint will not be bent too much when the legs are landed for the side splits. It also helps to avoid injuries to the knee joints and ligaments. If there is difficulty in landing both legs at the same time, land the left leg first and then rub the right leg across the ground for the splits. No matter how this is done, warm-up exercises are needed for the splits. Keep the chest out, back erect, and head up. Keep both arms straight and stretch them outward. Keep balance.

32. Sweeping Punch with Bow Step

(1) Keep the body weight up. Press the legs down, bend the knees and jump up, feet together and heels raised.

Fig. 3-78

While jumping up, swing the arms upward simultaneously, bend the elbows and withdraw them to the front of the chest. Change the right palm into fist and keep the left palm close to the right fist, fingers up. Thrust the chest out, drop the waist and look ahead. (Fig. 3-79)

(2) Shift the body weight forward, move the left foot forward, and bend both legs to half squat. At the same time, turn the trunk slightly to the right. Swing the right arm obliquely downward and backward in a curved shap, fist eye forward. Swing the left arm upward to the forward left, both arms straight. Then swing the right arm. Shift the body weight further to the right. Look at the right fist. (Fig. 3-80)

(3) Shift the body weight to the forward left, straighten the right leg, and bend the left leg to half squat to form the left bow step. At the same time, swing the right fist forcefully from the right obliquely to the upper left, and

slap the left palm with the back of the hand obliquely above the head. Bend the left arm slightly, straighten the right arm, and lean the trunk forward to the left. Look at the hands. (Fig. 3-81)

Essentials: While jumping up from the splits, make sure that the thighs and the right knee have lower pressure, and that there is coordination between raising the waist and swinging the arms. The movements of bending the knees and withdrawing the legs should be quick. Tighten up the body and close the arms. In Fig. 3-80, move the left foot forward before swinging the right arm and shifting the body weight to the right. The range of arm swinging should be wide to form a sharp contrast to Fig. 3-79. The sweeping punch should be executed by swinging the fist upward obliquely in curved shape, fist eye facing obliquely down and power applied to the fist face. Relax and lower the right shoulder. Straighten the right leg. The movements should be executed first slowly and then quickly, and neatly.

33. Sweeping Backward with Hands Support

(1) Bend the left leg to full squat and lay the right leg flat on the ground, right tiptoes inward. Bend the trunk forward and turn it to the right with both palms on the ground under the right leg. Turn the left arm inward, and the right arm outward, and turn the wrists to the right so that move the fingers as far backward as possible. Look obliquely down. (Fig. 3-82)

(2) Pivot on the ball of the left foot, continue to twist and turn the body backward to the right, and sweep around 360 degrees with the right sole close to the ground. Support the body with both hands on the ground. Look down obliquely. (Fig. 3-83)

Essentials: In executing the sweeping movement, keep the right knee straight and stretch the leg, heel on the

Fig. 3-79　　　　　　Fig. 3-80

Fig. 3-81

Fig. 3-82　　　　　Fig. 3-83

ground. Bend the left leg to full squat, buttocks close to the left heel. At the same time, keep the back erect and the hips down so as to prevent the buttocks from being raised or the body from rising while sweeping. There is no pause in Fig. 3-82. At the very beginning, efforts should be made to twist the waist and keep the hips down. The sweeping should be quick. The movements of turning the body with hands on the ground and leg sweeping should be connected and coordinated.

34. Turning Body and Threading Palm with Crouch Step

(1) Turn the body to the right, and shift the body weight to the right. Straighten the left leg and bend the right leg, tiptoes outward. At the same time, push the ground with both hands, swing the right arm from below to the upper right, and raise the left arm on the left side of the body, both arms straight with thumbs up. Look

forward to the right. (Fig. 3-84)

(2) Turn the trunk to the right, raise the body weight, straighten the right leg, and move the left leg towards the right foot and heel raised. At the same time, swing the right arm upward and backward, and the left arm downward, forward and upward, both arms straight. Extend the left shoulder and look ahead. (Fig. 3-85)

(3) Pivot on the ball of the right foot and turn 90 degrees to the right. Stand on the right leg, and continue to move the left leg, tiptoes on the ground, legs close to each other. Shift the body weight slightly to the right leg. Swing the left arm upward and to the right while turning the body, and press it down obliquely before the right shoulder, fingers backward and palm facing down. Swing the right palm downward, bend the elbow and withdraw it to the right side of the waist. Look ahead to the right. (Fig. 3-86)

(4) Stand on the right leg, bend the left leg and raise it, shank obliquely down and turned inward, and instep flat. Thrust the right palm forward and obliquely upward to the right over the back of the left palm, palm facing up. Bend the left elbow and withdraw the palm to under the right upper arm, palm facing down. Look ahead to the right palm. (Fig. 3-87)

(5) Move the left foot to the left side, leg straight, bend the right leg to the bow step and then to full squat for the crouch step. Thread the left palm close to the body forward and downward, turn the right arm inward and raise it on the right side of the body, both arms straight with thumbs up. Lean the trunk to the left side. Keep the chest out and drop the waist. Look ahead to the left. (Fig. 3-88)

Essentials: While turning the body and swinging the arms, keep the arms straight and swing them simultaneously. The range of swinging should be large and

Fig. 3-84

Fig. 3-85

Fig. 3-86

Fig. 3-87   Fig. 3-88

the limbs should be fully extended. In Fig. 3-86 and 3-87, try your best to raise the body up. In forming the crouch step, bend the right leg while landing the left leg, turn the body slightly to the right to form the bow step and then shift the body weight, turning the body slightly to the left to form the crouch step. Be sure not to land the left foot at once for the crouch step; otherwise, it is not easy to stand firmly, the changing body techniques can not be demonstrated, and the implications of attack and defence for the movements cannot be shown. Thread the palm close to the inner side of the left leg, and the outer edge of the palm across the left instep, with the force on the tips of the fingers. In the whole process of the movements, stress should be laid on the range of the movements and the clear distinction between their rise and fall. The movements should not be too quick. For the movements of the left palm in Fig. 3-87, see Fig. 3-56.

35. Pushing Palm with Snap Kick

(1) Shift the body weight to the left, straighten the right leg forcefully, and bend the left leg forward. Continue to thread the left palm forward to the left and raise the right arm horizontally on the back, both arms straight with thumbs up. Lean the trunk forward to the left. Look ahead to the left. (Fig. 3-89)

(2) Raise the body weight, turn the body to the left, straighten the right leg, heel slightly raised, and slip it a small step forward. Straighten the left leg and bend the knee slightly. Swing the right arm downward and forward, arm straight with the palm facing up. Bend the left elbow and withdraw the palm to the left side of the body, palm facing up. Lean the trunk slightly forward. Look ahead. (Fig. 3-90)

(3) Stand on the left leg, bend the right leg and raise it up first and then quickly snap it forward forcefully, instep flat. At the same time, push the left palm forward quickly, fingers up to form a standing palm. Bend the right elbow, swing the right palm backward and withdraw it to the right side of the waist, palm facing up. Look ahead. (Fig. 3-91)

Essentials: While snapping the leg, there must be a process of first bending and then stretching, and the snapping of the shank must be clear, quick and forceful and power applied to the tiptoes. The lowest level should be the horizontal level and the highest should not exceed the waist level. This is for releasing the power. The supporting leg must be straight. Avoid having a strong snapping and kicking leg and a weak supporting leg, arched back and loose hips. In pushing the left palm forward, relax the right shoulder, give the elbow joint the backward pulling force after the right elbow is bent and withdrawn, in coordination with the left palm, so as to show the power of the movements.

Fig. 3-89

Fig. 3-90   **Fig. 3-91**

36. Double Palm Push with Legs Crossed

Lower the body weight and shift it forward, bend the left leg, and move the right foot forward, tiptoes slightly inward. Bend the right leg quickly to half squat, bend the left leg, and raise it forward, left instep tightly against the inner side of the right knee for the back cross-legged balance. At the same time, turn the body to the left and push the right palm forward to the right quickly. Bend the left elbow first and then push the left palm from the chest to the left side of the body, both arms straight, fingers up and the left palm slightly higher than the right. Lean the trunk slightly forward to the right. Look ahead over the right palm. (Fig. 3-92)

Essentials: Before landing the right foot, bend the left leg to half squat. Before executing the back cross-legged balance, there must be a process of bending the knee to half squat. Upper limb movements should be completed

Fig. 3-92

simultaneously with the execution of the back cross-legged balance. In pushing the palms, the main stress is laid on the right palm. It is not necessary to swing the left palm backward forcefully. The pushing should be quick and the force point is on the outer edge of the palm. Stand firmly on the right leg. Place the left foot tightly on the right leg and exert force slightly forward. Pause for two or three seconds after this movement.

37. Turn Body, Press Palm and Punch with Bow Step

(1) Move the left foot crosswise to the left, shift the body weight to the left, and bend both legs to half squat, right heel raised. Turn the body slightly to the left, twist the waist, tighten up the hips, knees inward, and the chest slightly in. Swing the right arm downward and turn it inward with the thumb facing down. Swing the left palm upward from the chest to the right shoulder with palm facing obliquely down. Look at the right palm. (Fig. 3-93)

(2) Twist the trunk to the left first, swing the right arm downward and to the upper right, and the left arm from below to the left side of the body. At the same time, stand on the left leg, bend the right leg and raise it forward, placing the right foot against the inner side of the left leg. Look ahead to the right. (Fig. 3-94)

(3) Continue to turn the body to the right, land the right foot half a step from the inner side of the left foot, stamp the foot and bend the knee, tiptoes slightly outward. Then move the left foot forward to the left and bend the knee to half squat. At the same time, swing the left palm upward, to the left and forward, arm straight. Bend the elbow, turn the arm inward and press it forward to the left, fingers to the right and palm facing down. Change the right palm into fist, turn the arm outward, bend the elbow and withdraw it to the right side of the waist, fist centre

up. Look forward over the left palm. (Fig. 3-95)

(4) Turn the body to the left, straighten the right leg forcefully, and bend the left leg to half squat to form the left bow step. At the same time, thrust the right fist quickly forward, arm straight and fist centre down. Change the left palm into fist, bend the elbow and withdraw the palm to the left side of the waist, fist centre up. Look ahead. (Fig. 3-96)

Essentials: The step movement after foot stamping in Fig. 3-94 to Fig. 3-95 is not a jump, but a step change. After stamping the right foot, move the left foot forward immediately with the foot close to the ground. The leg should not be raised high before stamping the left foot. There is a semi-horse-riding step before the bow step after stamping the foot. This is good for releasing the power in the heel kick and punch. Thrusting the fist must be based on the use of the power from turning the hips, kicking with the heel and turning the right heel outward. While swinging the right arm, extend the shoulder forward, especially when the body is turned to the left. In Fig. 3-93, the body parts should be tightened up, while in Fig. 3-94, the body parts should be extended to fully display the body techniques of opening and closing. No pause after this movement.

38. Cross Kick

Continue from the previous movement. Shift the body weight forward, straighten the left leg and stand on it, and swing the right leg quickly forward and upward, instep flat. Swing the left arm forward and upward, fingers to the right, and slap the right instep quickly with the right palm. Bend the right arm and withdraw the fist to the right side of the waist, fist centre facing up. Look at the left palm. (Fig. 3-97)

Fig. 3-93   Fig. 3-94

Fig. 3-95   Fig. 3-96

Fig. 3-97

Essentials: Straighten the supporting leg, and keep the hips upright and the back straight. In slapping the instep, the palm must be horizontal. In moving the right leg, keep it straight and the hips in so as to make the slapping accurate and loud. Relax the shoulders, and pull the right elbow back, with no pause after the movement.

39. Punching with Bow Step

Bend the left leg to half squat to form the bow step, and move the right leg backward, tiptoes inward and leg straight. At the same time, thrust the right fist forward, arm straight with fist centre down. Change the left palm into fist, bend the elbow and withdraw the fist to the left side of the waist, fist centre facing up. Look ahead. (Fig. 3-96)

Essentials: While bending the left leg, move the right foot backward. In landing the right foot, exert force to the shank and the outer side of the foot. The backward landing must be quick, and powerful. The cross kick is a high movement while the punch with bow step is a low movement. There must be a clear distinction between the rise and fall in the two movements; the bending and stretching of the left leg are particularly important. Thrusting the right fist and landing the backward foot should be completed simultaneously and in coordination. This movement should immediately follow the previous one and be connected with the following movement without any pause.

40. Turn About Face, Push Elbow with Bow Step

Continue from the previous movement. Pivot on the balls of both feet, and turn the body to the right. At the same time, straighten the left leg, heel outward, bend the right leg to half squat, heel inward, to form the bow step. While turning the body, change the left fist into palm, fingers up, bend the elbow and swing it upward to the left shoulder. Bend the right elbow and swing the fist to the left shoulder, fist face tightly against the left palm and fist centre down. Swing the left palm and right fist horizontally to the right simultaneously, so as to push the elbow to the right. Lean the trunk slightly forward to the right. Look ahead to the right. (Figs. 3-98A, B)

Essentials: In pushing the elbow, the movement should be executed horizontally from left to right, with force on the elbow joint. Place the elbow at shoulder level, and relax and drop the shoulders. The force point should be accurate. Turning the body, kicking with the heel, pivoting on the heels and turning the hips should coordinated with pushing the elbow and releasing the power. At the same time, attention should be paid to the control of power applied to the execution of the movements. Avoid over-

Fig. 3-98A　　　　Fig. 3-98B

exertion of power and stiff movements. There is no pause from Exercise Thirty-seven to Exercise Forty. At the same time, do not overlook the relation between the rise and fall in the quick connections, the range of opening and closing, and rhythms. Avoid any ambiguity and sloppiness in the movements.

41. Upper Block and Punch with Bow Step

(1) Shift the body weight to the left, and raise the body. Turn the body to the left and bend the left leg, tiptoes outward. Straighten the right leg with the turning of the body, heel raised and legs crossed. Change the right fist into palm and swing it downward and forward to the right, the left arm downward and to the left side of the body, both arms straight and the thumbs up. Shift the body weight forward. Look ahead. (Fig. 3-99)

(2) Continue to shift the body weight forward to the

right, and stand on the left leg, heel raised. Bend the right leg and raise the knee forward to the right, right foot close to the inner side of the left leg. Continue to swing the right arm upward and to the left shoulder, and the left arm downward and to the right under the right upper arm, arms crossed, palms facing down and right arm above. Lower the head and look at the right palm. (Fig. 3-100)

(3) Shift the body weight to the right, move the right foot to the right, bend the knee to half squat to form the bow step, and straighten the left leg, whole foot on the ground. At the same time, swing the right arm downward and to the right, arm straight and thumb facing up. Bend the left elbow and swing the arm downward. Change the left palm into fist and withdraw it to the left side of the waist, fist centre facing up. Lean the trunk slightly to the right. Look ahead over the right palm. (Fig. 3-101)

(4) Keep the bow step, and the trunk upright. At the same time, swing the right arm upward, snap the wrist and place the right palm above the head to the right. At the same time, thrust the left fist obliquely forward to the left, arm straight, fist centre down. Turn the head to the left, and look ahead over the left fist. (Fig. 3-102)

Essentials: In swinging the arms, keep them straight and the range of swing should be wide. Straighten the left leg as much as possible, with the trunk fully extended. The closing of the arms should be tight. When turning the body to the left, the body weight should be shifted forward to the right so that the movements are closely connected and smooth. In Fig. 3-101, the speed for the moving of the foot forward should be quicker than the swinging of the right arm. This makes the movements stable and makes it easier to swing the right arm. Shift the trunk to the right forward as much as possible, and stretch the right arm as far as possible. In executing the movements in Fig. 3-102, raise

Fig. 3-99   Fig. 3-100

Fig. 3-101   Fig. 3-102

the right arm and the body fully upward. The left fist and left leg do not form a straight line. Therefore, in thrusting the left fist, turn the waist slightly to the right to increase the intensity of the movement. Turn the head to the left powerfully. In Fig. 3-99 and Fig. 3-100, in swinging the right arm to the left, just follow the movement with the eyes (first look up at the right palm and then lower the head) so as to demonstrate the close coordination among the hands, eyes, body and steps.

42. Hacking Fist with Front Toe Step

(1) Turn the body to the left, shift the body weight forward to the left, bend the left leg to half squat, and straighten the right leg to form the left bow step. Change the right palm into fist and swing it from right downward and obliquely forward, arm straight and fist eye facing up. Change the left fist into palm, bend the elbow and place it at the inner side of the right upper arm, palm facing down. Bend the trunk forward slightly and look at the right fist. (Fig. 3-103)

(2) Turn the trunk slightly to the right and shift the body weight to the right. Stand on the right leg, and move the left foot ahead of the right foot after straightening the left leg, instep flat and tiptoes on the ground. Turn the right arm inward, continue to swing the right fist upward and to the right forcefully, and hack down, arm straight and fist eye up. Swing the left palm upward, snap the wrist and place the palm above the head to the left. Turn the head to the right and look ahead to the right. (Fig. 3-104)

Essentials: In Fig. 3-103, the shift of the body weight and the swing of the fist should not be too quick while the hacking must be quick and powerful. When moving the left foot ahead of the right foot, bend the shank slightly before snapping the leg forward, tiptoes or ball of the foot

Fig. 3-103   Fig. 3-104

on the ground. In forming the front toe step, the left heel should be slightly raised and the right solid, both legs straight. Keep the chest out, waist erect, hips upright and left palm up. Lean the trunk slightly to the right. In hacking the arm should be bent first and then straight, with the power reaching the fist wheel.

Part Three

43. Butterfly with Skipping Step

(1) Move the left foot one step crosswise to the left, tiptoes outward, turn the body to the left, left leg slightly bent, and straighten the right leg, heel raised and legs crossed. Change the right fist into palm and swing it from right to forward left and upward. Bend the left arm and raise it up to cross with right forearm above the head,

right arm outside and fingers of both hands up. Look ahead. (Fig. 3-105)

(2) Pivot on the ball of the left foot, continue to turn the body to the left, move the right foot forward to the right, tiptoes inward, ball on the ground and both legs slightly bent. Continue to swing the right arm from left backward and to the right to describe a small curve over the head and then to the right side of the body. At the same time, swing the left arm to the right, forward and to the left to describe a small curve over the head, arm naturally bent. Look ahead to the left. (Fig. 3-106)

(3) Continue to turn the body slightly to the left, shift the body weight backward, bend the right leg slightly and stand on it. Press the left leg on the ground forcefully and then swing it up backward, leg straight and foot lower than the buttocks. Continue to swing the left arm to the left backward to describe a small curve over the head, and then bend the elbow and withdraw it to the right shoulder, palm facing down. Swing the right arm downward and raise it naturally and obliquely backward to the right side of the body. Bend the trunk forward and look obliquely down. (Fig. 3-107)

(4) Continue to shift the body weight backward, straighten the right foot on the ground forcefully and then jump up to skip half a step, ball of the right foot on the ground first and then the whole foot. Bend the knee to half squat. Then move the left foot obliquely backward, ball on the ground. Keep both arms in the same position. Bend the trunk forward and twist it slightly to the right. Look down obliquely. (Fig. 3-108)

(5) Turn the body to the left and backward, trunk bend, shift the body weight to the left leg and bend it to half squat. Straighten the right leg against the ground, heel raised. At the same time, swing the arms to the left

| Fig. 3-105 | Fig. 3-106 |

| Fig. 3-107 | Fig. 3-108 |

horizontally and forcefully and stretch the left arm while turning the body. Look ahead to the left. (Fig. 3-109)

(6) Continue to turn the trunk to the left, body bent horizontally and straighten the left leg and raise the body. After stepping on the ground, swing the right leg backward and upward quickly, leg straight and instep flat. Swing the arms horizontally to the left together with the turning of the body. Look ahead. (Fig. 3-110)

(7) Continue to turn the trunk to the left, body bent horizontally, and continue to swing the right leg upward, and to the right in a curve in the air. After stepping on the ground, swing the left leg to the left and backward quickly. Swing the arms horizontally to the left, keep the chest out, raise the head, extend the abdomen and swing the legs backward. Look ahead. (Figs. 3-111A, B)

(8) Land the right foot forward naturally, and land the left foot to the left after swinging it backward to the left, ball on the ground. Bend the legs slightly for a buffer. Swing the left arm horizontally, and withdraw it to the front of the body, raising the right arm obliquely backward on the right side of the body, arm straight and both palms facing down. Raise the trunk slightly. Look ahead. (Fig. 3-112)

Essentials: There is a great degree of difficulty in executing the butterfly. There are different requirements for the different movements, from the running, stepping, leg swinging, jumping and landing. Failure to do any link well is bound to affect the integrity of the exercise. In order to describe the requirements and points for attention, I will explain each movement. The arm swinging in Fig. 3-105 and Fig. 3-106 is in fact the waving of hands like clouds with body turn. The range of swinging the arms should not be wide and should be limited to the description of horizontal curves over the head. The order of applying

Fig. 3-109   Fig. 3-110

Fig. 3-111A   Fig. 3-111B

Fig. 3-112

power is first to the right arm and then to the left arm. In Fig. 3-107 and Fig. 3-108, do not execute the backward skipping step after the left leg is swung backward and upward, but step quickly with the right leg for the skipping step by using the force from swinging the left leg upward. Do not jump too high from the ground. By skipping a small step on the ground, it is easier to connect the following exercise. In Fig. 3-108, twist and turn the trunk consciously to the right after landing the left foot. Swing the left arm back to the right shoulder in order to increase the range of swinging. Relax a bit, and collect power before executing the movements in Fig. 3-109. The movements from Fig. 3-105 to Fig. 3-108 form the stage of turning the body and running. At this stage, attention should be paid to turning the body. The skipping step should be executed quickly and forcefully, and the inertia from running should be fully used to increase the power and height for the jump. In executing Fig. 3-109 and Fig. 3-110, several points should be made: The speed and power of bending the trunk and turning the body to the left backward should be great, and the waist should produce "twisting power" that bursts out suddenly. At the same time, the arms should coordinate with the turning of the body, swing to the left forcefully, left arm leading. While bending the trunk horizontally, straighten the left leg forcefully and jump up. On the one hand, turn the waist horizontally; on the other, raise the waist and energy. Both are indispensable. In Fig. 3-111 and Fig. 3-112, attention should be first paid to the complete posture of the Butterfly, in which the arms are swung separately to the two sides. Keep the legs apart, instep flat, chest out, head raised, and abdomen extended. It is required that the movements be high and floating while the landing is light and firm.

44. Turn Body with Hook Hand and Slap Palm

(1) Turn the body 180 degrees to the left, and shift the body weight to the left leg. While turning the body, land the left foot, heel first on the ground, and pivoting on the heel, turn the tiptoes outward. Bend the leg slightly, and straighten the right leg, heel raised and legs crossed. While turning the body, swing the right arm upward, to the right and forward, arm turned inward and the bend between the thumb and forefinger facing down. At the same time, bend the left arm, and withdraw the palm under the right upper arm, palm facing down. Lean the trunk to the right side. Look ahead to the right. (Fig. 3-113)

(2) Continue to shift the body weight forward to the right, move the right foot closely forward to the right, leg slightly bent, and straighten the left leg. At the same time, swing the right arm from below to the left, upward, to the

right and obliquely upward. Keep arm straight, and the left arm downward and to the left side of the body, thumbs facing up. Look ahead to the right. (Fig. 3-114)

(3) Continue to shift the body weight to the right and move the left foot backward behind the right foot, ball on the ground and legs crossed and bent to half squat. At the same time, continue to swing the left arm upward and bend the elbow in front of the body, and swing it to the front of the right shoulder, fingers up (see Fig. 3-93). Turn the right arm inward with thumb facing down, and raise the straight arm on the right side of the body. Bend the trunk slightly forward and look ahead. (Fig. 3-115)

(4) Turn the body 180 degrees to the left, right tiptoes inward. Straighten the right leg and stand on it, and move the left foot half a step crosswise to the left. At the same time, swing the left arm from below upward and to the left, and the right arm downward, upward and to the right side of the body. Keep both arms straight, left palm facing down and right palm facing up, and lean the trunk to the right. Look ahead over the right palm. (Fig. 3-116)

(5) Pivot on the ball of the left foot, turn the body to the left, draw the right foot to the inner side of the left foot, and bend both knees to full squat, heels slightly off the ground. At the same time, continue to swing the right arm upward, forward and downward. Pat the ground with the palm, and swing the left arm downward, backward and upward to form a backhand hook. Bend the trunk forward and look at the ground in the front. (See Fig. 3-41)

Essentials: When turning the body and swinging the arms, keep both arms straight and close to the body to form vertical circles. Moving the feet forward and backward in Fig. 3-113 to Fig. 3-115 should be quick and should connect and coordinate closely with the swinging of the arms. When forming the hook and patting the ground,

Fig. 3-113   Fig. 3-114

Fig. 3-115   Fig. 3-116

keep the knees somewhat apart so that the trunk can be bent forward, thrust the chest out and drop the waist. The patting should not be too far from the body.

45. Side Sole Kick

(1) Turn the body to the right, and, at the same time, move the right foot obliquely forward before the left foot, tiptoes outward, legs crossed and knees bent to half squat. Swing the right arm to the left, forward and upward, and change the left hook hand into palm swinging it to the left and horizontally to the front of the body. Bend both elbows and cross the palms at wrist in front of the chest, fingers up and right palm outside. Look ahead to the left. (Fig. 3-117)

(2) Straighten the right leg and stand on it. Flex the left foot and turn it inward, then bend the knee to the left, raise it and kick forward to the upper left forcefully. Push both arms simultaneously to the two sides of the body, fingers forward. Lean the trunk to the right side and look at the left foot. (Fig. 3-118)

Essentials: When moving the right foot forward, do not be impatient to raise the other foot to kick, but stand on it firmly, pause a bit and even form the front cross step and stamp it to increase the impetus. In kicking with the left leg, first bend the leg and then stretch it, straighten the knee, open the hips and kick forcefully, with the power on the heel. Do not bend the trunk forward or backward. The kicking and the pushing of the palms should be completed simultaneously.

46. Inside Slap Crescent Kick

(1) Move the left foot obliquely backward to the left, tiptoes outward. Then shift the body weight to between the two legs and straighten the right leg, heel raised. Keep the thumb of the left palm apart, facing down, and swing the

Fig. 3-117   Fig. 3-118

palm slowly to the upper left. Change the right palm into fist, bend the elbow and withdraw it to the right side of the waist, fist centre up. Look at the left palm. (Fig. 3-119)

(2) Turn the body to the left, shift the body weight to the left leg and stand on it. Swing the right leg and kick to the right, upward and to the left, instep flat and inward, and both legs straight. Slap the ball of the right foot quickly with the left palm. Look at the left palm. (Figs. 3-120A, B)

Essentials: Landing the left foot should be connected with the swinging and kicking of the right leg. Do not be too impatient in turning the body to the left, but turn the body together with the swinging of the right leg. The movements should be coordinated and natural. In executing the inside kick, swing the leg from upper right to left in the shape of a Chinese fan, both legs straight, waist erect, hips upright, and head up. Relax the shoulders when

Fig. 3-119

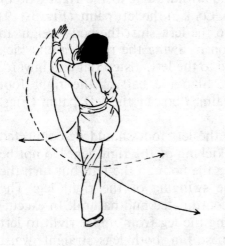

Fig. 3-120A   Fig. 3-120B

patting. The patting should be quick, accurate and loud.

47. Pushing Palm with Hooked Hand and Bow Step

Continue to turn the body to the left. After swinging the right leg to the left and downward, bend the knee, withdraw it to the inner side of the left leg, and then land the foot backward, leg straight. Bend the left leg to half squat to form left bow step. At the same time, change the right fist into palm and push it from the waist side forward, fingers up. Swing the left arm downward and backward to form a backhand hook, point up. Keep both arms straight, lean the trunk forward and look ahead. (Fig. 3-121)

Essentials: Bend the shank down first after slapping the right leg. In forming the bow step, bend the left leg while landing the right foot, and exert force to the outer side of the right foot. In pushing the palm, special attention should be paid to relaxing the left shoulder and keeping the hips upright, so that the whole movement is executed with care and force. Forming the bow step, pushing the hand and forming the hook hand should be well-coordinated.

48. Pressing Palm with Body Turn and Punching with Bow Step

(1) Raise the body weight, straighten the left leg, straighten the right leg and slip it a small step back to the left foot. At the same time, turn the body to the right, swing the right arm upward, and to the right, and change the left hook into palm. Swing it downward and to the left side of the body, both arms straight. Keep the trunk erect, but slightly to the left side. Look ahead to the right. (Fig. 3-122)

(2) Continue to turn the body 180 degrees to the right, bend the right leg and withdraw it half a step to the inner side of the left foot. Stamp the foot, bend the knee to half

squat and stand on it. Bend the left leg and raise it forward to the left, left foot against the back side of the right knee. While turning the body to the right, swing the left arm upward and to the left forward. Press the left palm downward, palm facing down, snap the wrist and turn the palm into a horizontal palm, fingers forward. Continue to swing the right arm, and change the right palm into fist, bend the elbow and withdraw it to the right side of the waist, fist centre up. Look ahead to the left. (Fig. 3-123)

(3) Move the left foot forward to the left, tiptoes slightly outward, to form the semi-horse-riding step. Shift the body weight to between the legs. Then bend the left leg to half squat, straighten the right leg forcefully, and turn the body to the left to form the left bow step. At the same time, thrust the right fist horizontally forward, change the left palm into fist, turn the arm outward, bend the elbow and withdraw it to the left side of the waist, fist centre up. Look ahead. (See Fig. 3-44)

Essentials: The body turn with foot stamping in Fig. 3-122 to Fig. 3-123 is not a jump-up, but a change of the step between the left and right foot. It is important to turn the body to the right and then stamp the foot and change the supporting leg. Speaking from the angle of attack and defence, the sudden change in the movements will catch the opponent unguarded, and it also helps beginners to release their force. After stamping the right foot, move the left foot immediately to form the semi-horse-riding stance and then execute the punch with bow step. It should not be done like this: thrusting the right fist forward while moving the left foot forward. In that case, the movements will not be coordinated and powerful. In thrusting the fist, use the power generated from turning the right heel outward, stamping the right leg, turning the hips, twisting the waist and extending the shoulders to support it. In

Fig. 3-121

Fig. 3-122

Fig. 3-123

forming the bow step, it is important to drop the hips and straighten the right leg. Do not raise the right heel nor turn up the outer side of the right foot.

49. Punching with Snap Kick

Raise the body weight, and stand on the left leg, bend the right leg, raise it up, and snap the leg forward quickly and forcefully, instep flat. At the same time, thrust the left fist quickly forward, fist eye up. Bend the right elbow and withdraw the fist to the right side of the waist. Look ahead. (Fig. 3-124)

Essentials: In snapping the leg, first bend the leg and then stretch it, bend the thigh and raise it level, and snap the shank forward neatly, quickly and forcefully, with the force on the tiptoes. Keep the leg straight, waist erect, hips upright, and head up. In punching, relax the shoulders and pull the right elbow backward so as to help the left fist release power.

50. Search-Sea Balance

(1) Move the right foot half a step forward, tiptoes precisely forward. Move the left foot to the inner side of the right foot with a follow-up step and keep them together, balls of both feet on the ground. Bend the legs to half squat. Change the left fist into palm, bend the elbow and swing it horizontally to the front of the right chest, palm facing down. At the same time, change the right fist into palm and withdraw it to the right side of the waist. Bend the trunk slightly forward. Look ahead. (Fig. 3-125)

(2) Stand on the right leg, and raise the left leg backward and up, instep flat and knees straight. At the same time, bend the trunk forward and thrust the right palm forward, fingers forward. Swing the left arm backward and raise it obliquely upward to the left. Look ahead. (Fig. 3-126)

Fig. 3-124

Fig. 3-125

Fig. 3-126

Essentials: Landing the right foot and moving the left foot to it in Fig. 3-125 can be executed as a small hopping step after you are skillful with the movements. The distant taken should not exceed one step. When taking the step, do not jump too high. The landing should be light, quick, firm and relaxed. The body weight is on the right leg, and the left foot is an empty step. In Fig. 3-126, do not bend the body too low, but raise the left leg backward as high as possible. Keep both legs and arms straight. Stand firm and pause for two to three seconds.

51. Single Slap Kick

(1) Move the left foot half a step obliquely behind the right foot, tiptoes on the ground, and keep the body weight at the right leg. Keep the trunk erect and turn it slightly to the right. At the same time, swing the right arm upward and place the right palm obliquely above the head. Swing the left palm from below to the left upward and to the front of the right shoulder, elbow bent and palm facing down. Look ahead. (Fig. 3-127)

(2) Turn the body slightly to the left, shift the body weight forward, and move the left foot half a step forward. Straighten the right leg, heel raised. At the same time, swing the left arm downward, forward and upward. Continue to swing the right arm backward, downward, upward and forward to slap the left palm with the back in front of the head, both elbows slightly bent. (See Figs. 3-16A, B). Look ahead. (Fig. 3-128)

(3) Stand on the left leg and swing the right leg quickly forward and upward with a kick, instep flat. At the same time, move the right arm forward to slap the right instep with the palm. Swing the left arm upward and raise it obliquely up to the left. Keep both arms straight and look at the right palm. (Fig. 3-129)

Fig. 3-127   Fig. 3-128

Fig. 3-129

Essentials: In Fig. 3-127, it is easier to stand firm when you turn the body to the right after landing the left foot. The range of raising the body up can be enlarged and the speed should be slower. The slapping of the two palms and moving the left foot forward should be completed at the same time. Therefore, the swing of the right arm should be done earlier than moving the left foot. Moreover, when the left foot is landed, the body weight should be shifted forward so as to raise the right leg. In Fig. 3-129, the slapping of the palms and foot should both be done close to and above the head. It should be quick, accurate and loud. Keep both legs straight. Do not arch the back and relax the hips in order to avoid moving the right leg too far forward. The rhythm of the movements should be quicker and quicker.

52. Raise Knee and Push Palm

(1) Turn the body 180 degrees to the left backward. At the same time, bend the left leg to squat, and straighten the right leg backward, tiptoes inward, to form the left bow step. Swing the right arm downward, forward and obliquely downward, arm straight, palm facing up. Bend the left arm, drop it down, and swing the left palm to the inner side of the right upper arm, palm facing downward. Lean the trunk slightly forward and look ahead over the right palm. (Fig. 3-130)

(2) Shift the body weight backward, bend the left leg and raise it up after stepping forcefully on the ground, shank inward and instep flat. Stand on the right leg and turn the trunk slightly to the right. At the same time, push the left palm forward to the left, bend the right elbow first and then push the right palm from the chest to the right, slightly higher than the left palm. Keep both arms straight, the fingers up and the trunk to the left. Look

ahead to the left. (Fig. 3-131)

Essentials: After finishing the single slap kick, immediately turn the body to the left. At this time, while landing the right leg, straighten the hips and the leg backward so that the movements will not be disconnected and relaxed. When arcing the right palm forward, it should not be too quick. On the other hand, the pushing of the palms to both sides should be quick and powerful. Keep the right leg straight and stand firm.

Part Four

53. Side Flip with Skipping Step

(1) Keep the body weight to the left forward, and move the left foot forward to the left, tiptoes outward, and immediately move the right foot obliquely before the left

Fig. 3-130   Fig. 3-131

foot for a front cross step, knee slightly bent. Straighten the left leg forcefully, keep both arms in the same position, and look ahead to the left. (Fig. 3-132)

(2) Continue to keep the body weight to the left forward, and turn the body slightly to the left. By making use of the forward impulsive force, jump up quickly after landing the right foot, and skip a half step forward. Bend the left leg immediately and swing it forward naturally, knee not higher than the hips. Whip the arms downward, and then backward and upward. Bend the trunk forward. Look down forward. (Fig. 3-133)

(3) After landing the right foot, move the left foot forward immediately, bend the legs to half squat, and press the left foot forcefully against the ground. Swing the right leg backward and upward quickly, leg straight and instep flat. Swing the arms forward naturally, and bend the trunk forward. Look at the ground. (Fig. 3-134)

(4) Continue to swing the right foot upward and to the right and swing the left leg upward quickly after pressing and leaving the ground, body in the air, both legs straight and instep flat. Swing both arms naturally in front of the body, thrust the chest out, raise the head and look at the ground. (Figs. 3-135A, B)

(5) Land the right foot after swinging the leg quickly, tiptoes forward, bend the knee to support the body, continue to swing the left leg downward in the air, and land it behind the right leg. Keep the trunk bent forward, and look at the ground obliquely. (Fig. 3-136)

Essentials: Running is an important link for the execution of the side flip in the air. Therefore, when running and skipping, the body weight must be shifted fully forward, and the moving of the feet must be nimble and quick. It is not necessary to think of the points for the flip too early. When pressing the left foot against the ground,

Fig. 3-132

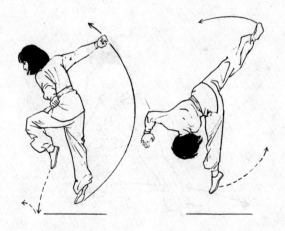

Fig. 3-133   Fig. 3-134

Fig. 3-135A   Fig. 3-135B

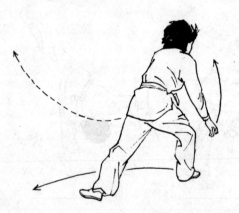

Fig. 3-136

swing the right leg upward quickly, raise the waist upward, gaining energy through breathing, and swing the arms forcefully to help raise the waist. The arms are swung in two ways: swing them from the front downward, backward and upward; or swing them from behind downward, forward and upward. Use of either method depends on which helps you to exert your force. There are no specific requirements. While in the air, the legs should be swung with the hips open and fully apart, and knees straight. When landing the feet after the flip, plant the right foot downward right under the body, tiptoes precisely forward. The landing should be light and stable.

54. Turn Body and Step Forward with Heel Kick and Punch

(1) Turn the body 180 degrees backward to the left, left tiptoes quickly turned outward, and move the right foot immediately forward, tiptoes slightly outward. Shift the body weight forward and straighten the left foot, heel raised. At the same time, swing the left arm downward and forward while turning the body, the thumb facing up. Raise the right arm obliquely backward to the right, both arms straight and left shoulder extended forward. Look ahead. (Fig. 3-137)

(2) Keep the body weight forward, move the left foot immediately forward, bend the leg slightly, and straighten the right leg, heel raised. At the same time, swing the right arm downward and forward, and turn the arm outward so that the palm faces up. Change the left palm into fist, bend the elbow, swing it backward and withdraw it to the left side of the waist, fist centre facing up. Look ahead. (Fig. 3-138)

(3) Stand on the left leg, bend the right leg, raise it up and then kick with the heel forward forcefully, right leg level, tiptoes up and body weight still forward. At the same

time, thrust the left fist forward quickly and extend the left shoulder. Change the right palm into fist, bend the elbow, swing it backward and withdraw it to the right side of the waist, fist centre facing up. Look ahead. (Fig. 3-139)

Essentials: The body turn and forward step should be closely connected. In straightening the legs, bend the knee and raise the thigh level, and go through a process of first bending and then stretching with the force exerted to the heel. In thrusting the fist, relax both shoulders, twist the waist, and extend the left shoulder. There is no pause in this movement, and the body weight is always kept forward. However, avoid raising the leg too low and turning the movement into a big step forward.

55. Punch with Right Bow Step

Land the right foot forward, bend the knee to half squat, and straighten the left leg to form the bow step. Turn the trunk slightly to the left, and thrust the right fist horizontally forward to the right. At the same time, turn the left arm outward, bend the elbow and withdraw the fist to the left side of the waist, fist centre facing up. Lean the trunk slightly to the right and look ahead over the right fist. (Fig. 3-140)

Essential: Bend the left leg while landing the right foot, right heel first on the ground and then the whole foot. Bend the legs to half squat. It should be noted that as soon as the right foot is landed, the bow step should be formed, and its length should be neither too big, nor too small. The punch must be quick and forceful, with the force reaching the fist face.

56. Bent Elbow with Bow Step

Shift the body weight to the left, turn the trunk slightly to the left, straighten the right leg forcefully, and bend the left leg to half squat to form the left bow step. At the same

Fig. 3-137

Fig. 3-138

Fig. 3-139

Fig. 3-140

time, swing the right arm horizontally forward and to the left. Bend the elbow and withdraw it to the right chest, fist centre facing down, and fist to elbow level. Withdraw the left fist to the left side of the waist, and lean the trunk slightly forward. Look ahead. (Fig. 3-141)

Essentials: In forming the left bow step, attention should be paid to coordination among thrusting the right heel out, turning the hips and twisting the waist when straightening the right leg. Before swinging the right arm horizontally forward, swing it slightly to the right, and then to the left, in order to increase the range and power of the swinging prior to the bending of the elbow. In forming the bow step, drop the hips, keep the waist erect, avoid raising the buttocks and twisting the hips to the left.

57. Hammer Fist with Feet Together

(1) Shift the body weight to the right, turn the trunk

to the right, bend the right knee and straighten the left leg, heel raised. Swing the left arm downward and forward, and the right arm horizontally to the right and backward, palm facing down and both arms straight. Look ahead. (Fig. 3-142)

(2) Keep the body weight between the two legs, and straighten both legs. Turn the trunk slightly over to the upper left. At the same time, turn the left arm inward so the thumb is down. Keep the thumb apart and continue to swing the arm upward slowly. Swing the right arm downward and backward to the right, arm straight and fingers down. Bend the trunk backward, thrust the chest out, and raise the head. Look at the left palm. (Fig. 3-143)

(3) Continue to turn the body to the left, shift the body weight to the left leg and stand on it, heel raised. After pressing the right leg on the ground, bend it quickly and raise it up, shank close to the inner side of the left leg. Continue to swing the left arm upward, to the left and downward to the left side of the body, palm facing obliquely down. Swing the right arm from below to the right and upward, and while swinging it to above the head, clench the fist. Look ahead. (See Fig. 3-26, but the direction of the movement should be left forward, the same as in Fig. 3-144)

(4) Land the right foot to the inner side of the left foot and stamp the ground with the whole foot, bending the leg to half squat. At the same time, turn the left arm outward, bend the elbow and withdraw it to the front of the body, palm facing up. Move the right fist down in front of the body, bending the knees and slapping the left palm with the fist back. Look ahead. (Fig. 3-144)

Essentials: In Figs. 3-142, 3-143, and 3-26, the range of the movements of the upper part of the body should be large. In swinging the left arm, extend the left shoulder,

Fig. 3-141   Fig. 3-142

Fig. 3-143   Fig. 3-144

chest and waist fully, and the movements should be connected and quick. When stamping, stamp the ground with the whole right foot and a loud sound. It should be completed simultaneously with the hammer drive. When squatting with the feet together, keep the knees close to each other, thrust the chest and drop the waist. Do not bend the trunk forward.

58. Front Kick with Forward Step

(1) Move the left foot obliquely forward, and straighten the right leg, heel raised. Change the right fist into palm, swing it forward and raise it obliquely up in front of the body. Swing the left arm from below backward to obliquely down. Look ahead. (Fig. 3-145)

(2) Shift the body weight forward and stand on the left leg. Flex the right foot and swing the leg quickly to kick forward and upward, close to the forehead. Swing the left arm upward and place the left palm above the head to the left. Swing the right arm downward and backward to behind the body to form a backhand hook, point up. Look ahead. (Fig. 3-146)

Essentials: The movements of moving the left foot forward and kicking with the right leg should be connected. When executing the front kick, keep both legs straight, and the hips upright for the suppoting leg in particular, so that the straightening of the left leg and the uplifting of the left arm should be identical. Keep the left heel on the ground. The kicking of the right leg should be light, nimble, quick and forceful. Keep the chest out, the abdomen in, and the body upright.

59. Part Palms with Empty Step

(1) Land the right foot backward, ball on the ground, and bend the left leg slightly. Swing the left arm downward, palm facing down. Change the right hook into palm,

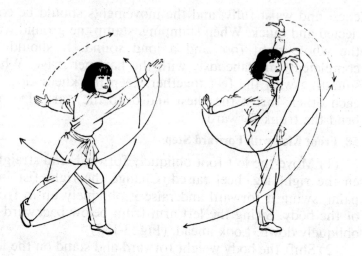

Fig. 3-145   Fig. 3-146

and swing it from below forward, and obliquely upward to slap the left palm with the back in front of the head. Look ahead. (Fig. 3-147)

(2) Shift the body weight backward, and stand on the right leg. After pressing the ground forcefully, bend the left leg and raise it forward, left foot against the inner side of the right leg. While slapping the palms, raise them over the head, palms facing forward. Look ahead. (Fig. 3-148)

(3) Bend the right leg to half squat, and quickly snap the left shank obliquely forward to the left, the inner side of the ball on the ground, and bend the leg slightly to form an empty step. At the same time, swing the palms apart to the lower left and upper right, and turn the arms outward so that the palms face up. Keep both arms straight and look ahead obliquely to the left. (Fig. 3-149)

Essentials: In executing Fig. 3-149, extend the body upward, both arms raised high, and immediately form the empty step. The squatting should be completed at one stroke, with a clear distinction between the high and the low. In forming the empty step the left foot should be empty while the right is solid. Thrust the chest out, drop the waist and avoid bending the trunk forward, slanting the body and forming oblique hips. The swinging apart of the palms and forming the empty step should be coordinated.

60. Press Palms with Feet Together

(1) Shift the body weight forward, move the left foot half a step forward, bend the leg forward and straighten the right leg. At the same time, move the left palm to describe a small curve to the left, bend the elbow and withdraw it to the side of the waist, palm facing up. Move the right palm downward, bend the elbow and withdraw it together with the left palm to the right side of the waist and then thrust them forward, both arms straight and palms facing up. Look ahead over the palms. (Fig. 3-150)

(2) Turn the body to the right, bend the right leg slightly, and straighten the left leg. Swing the right arm downward and obliquely upward, and raise the left arm obliquely down. Look at the right palm. (Fig. 3-151)

(3) Shift the body weight forward to the left, stand on the left leg, and move the right foot quickly to the inner side of the left foot. At the same time, swing both arms upward, and press the palms from the ears down to the respective side of the hips, elbow slightly bent, palms facing down. Turn the head to the left and look ahead to the left. (Fig. 3-152)

Essentials: From Fig. 3-150 to Fig.3-151, the movements should be slowed down properly. In pressing the palms with the feet together, the movement should be quick and neat. It should be completed simultaneously

Fig. 3-147

Fig. 3-148

Fig. 3-149

Fig. 3-150

Fig. 3-151

Fig. 3-152

Fig. 3-153

with the abrupt turning of the head to the left. In pressing the palms, keep them apart and exert the force to the roots of the palms. Thrust the chest out and the abdomen in.

61. Finishing Form

Stand still with feet together, and keep both arms straight and down, fingers together against the outer sides of the thighs. Look ahead. (Fig. 3-153)

IV. Practical Techniques for Duel Practice

Duel is one of the important exercises in the Chinese Wushu. It is an exercise in which two or more persons practise attack and defence skills according to the arranged routines on the basis of the individual practice. The duel routines are composed of combat methods, including kicking, striking, throwing, catching and use of weapons in line with the principle of reasonable attack and defence techniques.

Through the duel practice, you can further understand the technical implications and actual combat uses of the movements in the individual practice routines and effectively improve the technical level of the individual practice movements. Moreover, as the duel routines are similar to actual combat, requiring the skill accuracy of the movements, both partners must cooperate well. It also helps to cultivate resourcefulness, bravery and quickness of Wushu enthusiasts.

Duel routines are classified into three categories: bare-handed duels, duels with weapons, and duels between armed and unarmed persons.

Bare-handed duel is a duel in which the opponents use the hand, leg and body techniques according to the rules of movements for attack, defence and counterattack. As the different schools of boxing have different styles and features, the forms and contents for the duels also vary. Chang Quan duel routines involve more running, leaping, jumping, tumbling and rolling movements; they are characterized by quickness and nimbleness.

Duel with weapons is a duel in which the opponents both use weapons for attack and defence, and each weapon has its own characteristics. For example, in playing with the sabre, one has to show bravery, fierceness, fortitude and quickness. While playing with the sword, one should display the softness in hardness, spryness and naturalness. In the duels with other weapons, there should be good coordination among the long, short, double and soft weapons.

A duel between bare hands and weapons is a duel in which one person uses a weapon and the other does not. In such duels, the routines are mostly arranged for the unarmed player to seize the weapon from his opponent; for example, to seize sabre, spear and double spears with bare hands. In the duels, the armed person is required to have a good mastery of his weapon and the unarmed player is required to know how to dodge quickly from attack and play his routines very skillfully.

In the following pages, I will describe two sets of practical Chang Quan routines (Bare-handed duels), for beginners.

First of all, in practising the duel routines, you should pay attention to the following points:

(One) The difference between individual practice and duel practice.

Duel practice is the continuation and extension of the individual practice, but has its own particularities. As it is a simulated duel exercise, not all the essential points of the individual practice routines can be copied into the duel routines. If the stances used in the routines for single practice are applied to the duel routines, the play will look obviously stiff and awkward. The leg techniques, such as kicks, and hand techniques, such as punches, cannot be as fierce and powerful as in the singles. On the one hand, you have to display your quickness, bravery and actual combat ability; on the other, you have to have the ability to control your movements so as not to hurt your opponents.

(Two) Follow the principles for the duel practice.

In the duels, it is necessary to stress the actual combat postures of the movements and the high concentration. In the course of the practice, not only must the partners show combat awareness in every movement, and look as if they are in actual combat, but they must also use accurate methods to ensure the opponent is not injured. Accurate methods mean that all movements are executed accurately to the desired positions. For example, when thrusting the fist horizontally forward, you must hit at the chest side or shoulder side, not the right chest of your opponent.

In practising the duels, the partners must keep proper distance between them. If they are too far from each other, the exercise looks loose and the method of attack and defence cannot be displayed. If they are too close, their limbs cannot be fully extended and the movements are affected. Moreover, the partners are required to coordinate their movements. If one plays slowly and the other plays quickly, injuries are apt to occur and the movements might be awkward. Therefore, in the course of the practice, both sides should keep good time for attack and defence in every form and exercise.

(Three) Use the practising method reasonably.

In practising the duel routines, apart from the training by the single practice method, you should also strengthen the training for the separate movements and for coordination. The practice for the separate movements is mainly intended to improve the technical level of the players' personal skills. For example, in Fig. 5-56 and Fig. 5-57, the fourth movement is the swinging kick of the right leg; B can practise this movement against other objects (not too high) repeatedly in order to achieve the accuracy and stability of the kick. In practising the coordination movements, the main stress is on how to attack and defend at the right time; for example, in Figs. 5-73 and 5-74, the 15th movement, Practical Exercises (II), when A executes the double horizontal punch and B lowers his head to dodge. This requires A to grasp the height, line and speed well, and B to complete the movement of lowering his head at the precise moment the sweeping punch comes from A. Sufficient practice for such coordination helps you to grasp the rules of movement and essential technical points for the duel exercises and improve the quality of the movements. This will make the movements look very real and will also effectively prevent injuries.

In order to learn the methods of attack, defence and counterattack in the duel routines, and gradually improve their movements, the beginners can use the following two methods.

1. Shout commands to A to complete the first movement of attack and then ask B to execute the corresponding movement of dealing with the attack. As the movements of the two partners—attack and defence in the routines—are connected and executed simultaneously, it is inevitable to find themselves too close to each other and their movements not fully extended. However, to enable beginners to understand the practical implications of every movement in the duel routines and execute the movements up to technical requirements, I still insist that they first use this method for practice.

2. On the basis of the first method, the two sides should each execute his own movements of attack, defence or counter-attack in the sequence of the complete routine after a command is issued. Movements should be executed first slowly and then quickly; at first not exerting force and later exerting force.

(Four) Decide the participants in the duels.

Two points should be made as to the selection of the partners in the duels.

1. The height difference should not be too large, in order to avoid the big difference in foot width between the partners and not affect the quality of completing the movements.

2. The partners should be equal in skills and technical levels. Through repeated practice, they can cooperate well and execute the movements with high proficiency.

(Five) Choose the practice ground and lighting correctly.

As there are often tumbling and rolling movements in the duel routines, the practise ground should be large, flat and soft so as to prevent injuries. If conditions permit, it is better to practise on a carpeted floor, or on a mat or lawn.

The lighting should not too dark, nor should it shine on the faces, or it will affect the line of sight and the completion of the movements.

(Six) Warm-up exercises

Warm-up exercises are intended to increase the stimulation of the central nervous system so that the function of the internal organs, joints and ligaments gradually adapt to the needs of the movements, and at the same time to prevent injuries. Before the duel exercises, run slowly, do bare-handed exercises or play games. The formal practice begins after all the parts of the body are warmed up to sweat slightly.

V. Practical Methods for Duel Practice

This set of practical Chang Quan exercises is divided into single and duel exercises. The duel exercises are done on the basis of the single exercises. First, the players practise singly to learn how to do the single exercises. Then, they practise together face to face, A the first ten movements, and B the second ten movements in the form of a duel. After they exchange the movements, they complete their 20 duel exercises. Beginners are allowed to shout commands. In the duel exercises, first execute the movements in the correct order.

Names of Exercises
1. Starting Form
2. Bow Step, Block and Spring Fist
3. Raise Knee and Brush Hand
4. Forward Step and Snap Kick
5. Horse-Riding Step and Horizontal Strike
6. Change to Jump, Press Palm, Bow Step and Punch
7. Backward Step, Side Bow Step and Hammer Strike
8. Bow Step, Block and Uppercut with Fist
9. Bow Step and Push Elbow
10. Feet Together and Fist Thrust
11. Side Bow Step, Push Elbow and Punch
12. Bow Step and Punch
13. Swing Leg, Bow Step and Press Palm
14. Downward Chopping Palm
15. Horse-Riding Step and Outward Parry
16. Heel Kick, and Push Palm with Bow Step
17. Twist Body, Upper Block and Side Snap Kick
18. Press and Hack Palm with Bow Step

19. Backward Step, Horse-Riding Step and Parry
20. Backward Step, Semi-Horse-Riding Step, Block
    and Downward Plunge
21. Bow Step and Push Palm
22. Closing Form

Illustrated Exercises

1. Starting Form

(1) Stand erect with feet together, arms straight by both sides, and thrust the chest out and the abdomen in. Look ahead. (Fig. 5-1)

(2) Stand erect with feet together, turn the arms outward and raise them horizontally to both sides, palms facing up. Look at the right palm. (Fig. 5-2)

(3) Continue to raise the arms upward, turn them inward when they are raised to the head level, and press them downward in front of the body to the abdomen level, palms facing down and fingers pointing to each other. Turn the head to the left and look ahead to the left. (Fig. 5-3)

2. Bow Step, Block and Spring Fist

(1) Move the right foot one step to the right side, bend the right leg at knee, and straighten the left leg. At the same time, turn the left arm outward and swing it from the left side upward, palm facing obliquely up. Change the right palm into fist, bend the elbow and withdraw it to the right side of the waist, palm facing up. Look at the left palm. (Fig. 5-4)

(2) When the left hand is raised to the shoulder level, bend the elbow down immediately, and change the palm into fist to parry to the right, forearm placed obliquely in front of the left chest and palm facing inward. At the same time, twist the waist to the right and withdraw the right fist to the waist side. Look at the left fist. (Fig. 5-5)

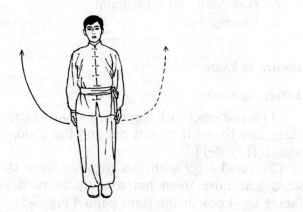

Fig. 5-1

Fig. 5-2   Fig. 5-3

(3) Pause a little in the preceding movement (no pause in the duel). Shift the body weight to the left, bend the left leg, and straighten the right leg to form the left bow step. Raise the left elbow up and pivot on the elbow to spring the back of the left fist obliquely upper left, fist eye facing up. Look at the left fist. (Fig. 5-6)

Essentials: When changing the right bow step into the left bow step, pivot on both feet to the left, right heel turned outward, with coordination between twisting the waist and turning the hips.

Implications for attack and defence: First parry the coming punch from the opponent, and then counterattack the opponent's head or face with the "spring fist."

3. Raise Knee and Brush Hand

Turn the trunk 90 degrees to the left. First change the right fist into palm and swing it from behind upward and forward to above the left wrist. While swinging the right palm, turn the left fist slightly inward, and immediately brush both hands downward and obliquely backward, changing the hands into hooks, tips up and both arms straight. At the same time, shift the body weight backward and stand on the right leg, bend the left leg and raise it up, shank obliquely down and slightly inward, and instep flat. (Fig. 5-7)

Essentials: The movement of brushing the hands should be forceful and completed simultaneously with the movement of raising the knee.

Implications for attack and defence: Brushing hand is to prevent the opponent from catching or holding your body parts, while raising the knee is to dodge from the opponent's attacking leg.

4. Forward Step and Snap Kick

Land the left foot half a step forward, shift the body weight immediately to the left leg and stand on it, and snap

Fig. 5-4

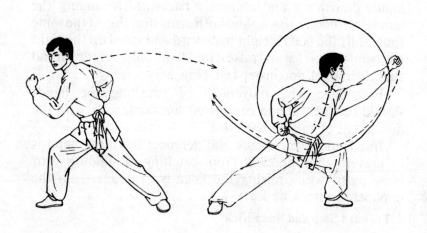

Fig. 5-5   Fig. 5-6

and kick forward immediately with the right leg. Look obliquely down. (Fig. 5-8)

Essentials: After landing the left foot, snap and kick with the right foot immediately. While kicking, keep the hips in, first flexing the leg and then stretching it. The movement should be quick and forceful.

Implications for attack and defence: The kick is directed at the knees of the opponent.

5. Horse-Riding Step and Horizontal Strike

Shift the body weight forward, land the right foot forward, then turn the body 90 degrees to the left, and bend both legs to half squat to form the horse-riding step. At the same time, change the right hook into fist, and swing it from behind horizontally to the right forward, with force applied to the fist eye, fist centre facing down. Change the left hook into fist and withdraw it to the left side of the waist, fist centre facing up. Look at the right fist. (Fig. 5-9)

Essentials: Land the right foot on the ground first and then turn the body, the hips and the feet. This movement and the horizontal striking should be well coordinated. Relax both shoulders.

Implications for attack and defence: From the angle of the height, this movement can be used to strike the head, chest or waist of the opponent horizontally.

6. Change to Jump, Press Palm, Bow Step and Punch

(1) Shift the body to the left and turn the body to the right at the same time. Pivot on the ball of the left foot, and stand on the left leg, bend the right leg and raise the knee up, shank inward. At the same time, change the left fist into palm, swing it from the left side upward, forward and downward, and press the palm obliquely downward in front of the body, palm centre facing down and fingers to the right. Bend the

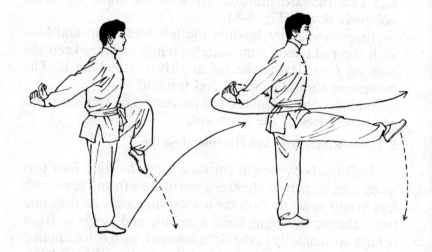

Fig. 5-7   Fig. 5-8

Fig. 5-9

right elbow and withdraw the fist to the right side of the waist. Look at the left palm. (Fig. 5-10)

(2) Pause a bit after the preceding movement (no pause in the duel exercise). Step forcefully on the ground with the left foot and jump up, and land the right foot quickly to the original position to support the body, tiptoes outward. Shift the body weight forward, and move the left foot immediately forward, bending the leg slightly to form the semi-horse-riding step. Immediately afterwards, bend the left leg forward, and straighten the right leg to form the left bow step. Thrust the right fist horizontally and straight forward from above the back of the left palm, bend the left elbow and withdraw the palm to under the right arm. Look ahead. (Fig. 5-11)

Essentials: First raise the right knee and withdraw the right fist. Then change to the jump and press the palm, and thrust the fist with bow step. All the movements must be closely connected.

Implications for attack and defence: "Change to the jump" is to dodge from the opponent's attacking kick; pressing the palm is to check the attacking fist or palm from the opponent. Draw it to your lower left and then attack the opponent's head with the punch.

7. Backward Step, Side Bow Step and Hammer Strike

After stepping on the ground, move the left foot one step backward, shift the body weight backward and turn the body slightly to the left. Bend the left leg and straighten the right leg, heel outward, to form the left bow step. At the same time, turn the right arm outward, bend the elbow and hammer down with the back of the right fist, with force applied to the fist back. Change the left palm into fist, bend the elbow and withdraw it to the left side of the waist. Look at the right fist. (Fig. 5-12)

Fig. 5-10

Fig. 5-11   **Fig. 5-12**

Essentials: The shift of the body weight backward must be quick. While hammering the fist down, drop the hips, and relax the shoulders.

Implications for attack and defence: Move the foot backward to prevent the opponent from kicking. Use the fist back or the outer side of the forearm to hammer the instep of the attacking foot of the opponent.

8. Bow Step, Block and Uppercut with Fist

Pivot on the balls of both feet, turn the body 90 degrees to the right, straighten the left leg, and bend the right leg to form the right bow step. At the same time, turn the right arm inward, move it upward in front of the body and place it above the head for block. Swing the left fist forward and upward in a curve to attack, with force applied to the fist face, elbow slightly bent and fist centre facing up. Look at the left fist. (Fig. 5-13)

Fig. 5-13

Essentials: The block and the attacking uppercut must be completed at the same time, and coordinated with the movement of turning the body to the right.

Implications for attack and defence: The right arm is used to block the opponent's attacking palm and the left fist is used to hit the opponent's abdomen.

9. Bow Step and Push Elbow

(1) Turn the right tiptoes outward and the body 90 degrees to the right, and move the left foot forward to the left, tiptoes forward. Bend both legs to half squat to form the semi-horse-riding step. Move the arms from above, bend the right elbow to the right backward and the left elbow to the left, and raise them horizontally in front of the chest, left fist centre facing down. Change the right fist into palm to form a standing palm, palm against the left fist. Look ahead to the left. (Fig. 5-14)

(2) Shift the body weight to the left, straighten the right leg forcefully, heel outward, and bend the left leg to half squat to form the left bow step. At the same time, push the left fist with the right palm, with the left elbow swinging horizontally to the left, and force applied to the elbow joint. Look ahead to the left. (Fig. 5-15)

Essentials: The elbow push must be coordinated with the straightening of the right leg and moving the waist and hips to the left.

Implications for attack and defence: Draw the attacking palm of the opponent backward to the right with both arms so that the opponent shifts his body weight to you, and then immediately push the elbow to attack the opponent's chest.

10. Feet Together and Fist Thrust

(1) Keep the bow step unchanged. Change the left fist into palm, pivot on the elbow joint and swing the palm

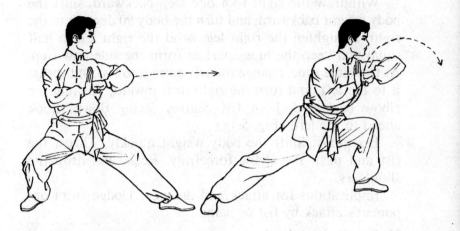

Fig. 5-14   Fig. 5-15

forward to the left and press it down. Change the right palm into fist, and while turning the forearm outward, bend the elbow backward and withdraw it to the right side of the waist. Look ahead to the left. (Fig. 5-16)

(2) Shift the body weight to the left, turn the body slightly to the left, and bend the left leg to half squat. Move the right foot forward to the inner side of the left foot and stamp the foot on the ground with a noise. At the same time, thrust the right fist forward. Bend the left elbow and withdraw the palm to the inner side of the right arm, fingers up. Look at the right fist. (Fig. 5-17)

Essentials: Punching and foot stamping must be completed at the same time. Thrust the chest out, drop the waist and extend the right shoulder forward.

Implications for attack and defence: Press the left palm forward to prevent the opponent from attacking with hand, and use the right fist to hit the opponent's abdomen.

11. Side Bow Step, Push Elbow and Punch

Withdraw the right foot one step backward, shift the body weight backward, and turn the body 90 degrees to the right. Straighten the right leg, bend the right leg to half squat and keep the hips apart to form the side bow step. At the same time, change the left palm into fist and thrust it to the left, and turn the right arm inward, pushing the elbow backward, both fist centres facing down. Look ahead to the left. (Fig. 5-18)

Essentials: Shift the body weight quickly. Thrust the fist and push the elbow forcefully. Relax and drop the shoulders.

Implications for attack and defence: Dodge from opponent's attack by fist or palm.

12. Bow Step and Punch

Shift the body weight to the left leg, and at the same time turn the body 90 degrees to the left, straighten the right leg quickly, and bend the left leg to half squat to form the left bow step. At the same time, turn the left fist outward, bend the elbow and withdraw the fist to the left side of the waist, fist centre up. Turn the right forearm outward, move from the waist side, then turn it inward, and thrust it forward quickly, fist centre down. Look ahead. (Fig. 5-19)

Essentials: The punch must be well coordinated with the power of the waist and legs. It must be quick and forceful. At the same time, relax the shoulders, drop the elbows and lower the hips.

Implications for attack and defence: Use the right fist to attack the opponent.

13. Swing Leg, Bow Step and Press Palm

(1) Raise the body slightly up, move the right foot half a step forward, heel on the ground and left leg slightly

Fig. 5-16   Fig. 5-17

Fig. 5-18

bent. At the same time, turn the left forearm inward, change the fist into palm, fingers up, and move it from the right chest upward to describe a curve to the head level. Bend the right elbow and withdraw the fist to the right side of the waist, fist centre up. Bend the trunk slightly backward. Look at the left palm. (Fig. 5-20)

(2) Immediately afterwards, clench the left hand into fist, and while turning the arm outward, bend the elbow and withdraw it to the left side of the waist, fist centre up. Change the right fist into palm, turn the forearm inward and press the palm forward, palm facing obliquely down and fingers up. At the same time, bend the left leg to squat, and slip the right foot on the ground obliquely backward to form the bow step, with force on the heel. Look at the right palm. (Fig. 5-21)

Essentials: When moving the right foot forward, bend the trunk slightly backward. Slipping the leg backward and pressing the palm forward must be well-coordinated. Relax the shoulders and lower the hips.

Implications for attack and defence: Use the left hand to block or catch the opponent's left fist, and use the right hand to hold up the opponent's left elbow or left shoulder. Press the opponent's left arm, and use the right heel to swing and kick at the opponent's left foot, so as to keep the opponent off balance.

14. Downward Chopping Palm

Change the right palm into fist, bend elbow and withdraw it to the right side of the waist, fist centre up. Turn the body to the right. Move the left foot to the inner side of the right foot, tiptoes or ball on the ground, and bend the legs to half squat with the right foot slightly ahead. At the same time, change the left fist into palm, and raise it up from the body side while turning the body, move it from the front of the body, and chop down fiercely, palm

Fig. 5-19   Fig. 5-20

Fig. 5-21

facing obliquely down. Look at the left palm. (Fig. 5-22)

Essentials: First turn the body to the right and withdraw the right fist, raise the left arm up and chop down with the palm. When withdrawing the left leg, the movement should be quick. Squatting and downward chopping should be completed simultaneously, neatly and cleanly.

Implications for attack and defence: Use the palm root or the forearm to parry off the opponent's kicking leg.

15. Horse-Riding Step and Outward Parry

Land the whole left foot, shift the body weight slightly to the right, and immediately move the right foot sideways to the right to form the horse-riding step. At the same time, bend the left arm and raise it obliquely up to form the standing palm, palm to the face level and palm facing forward. Look ahead to the left. (Fig. 5-23)

Essentials: Bending the elbow and raising it should be quick. Continue to parry towards behind the head.

Implications for attack and defence: Use the left palm or forearm to parry off the fist of the opponent attacking the head, chest or waist horizontally.

16. Heel Kick, and Push Palm with Bow Step

(1) Turn the left tiptoes outward, and turn the body 90 degrees to the left, shift the body weight to the left leg and stand on the left leg. Raise the right leg, foot flexed, and kick forward, to the knee level. At the same time, change the left palm into fist, bend the elbow and withdraw the fist to the left side of the waist, fist centre up. Look at the right foot. (Fig. 5-24)

(2) Continue to shift the body weight forward, land the right foot forward, bend the knee to half squat to form the bow step. At the same time, turn the body slightly to the left, change the right fist into palm, and push it forward from the waist side, fingers up. Look ahead to the right. (Fig. 5-25)

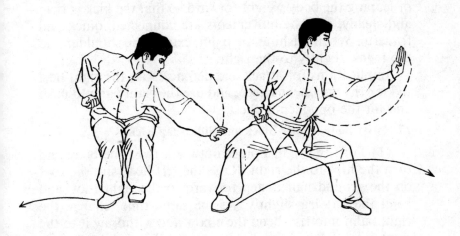

Fig. 5-22   Fig. 5-23

Fig. 5-24   Fig. 5-25

Essentials: While connecting the heel kick and push palm with bow step, attention should be paid to the degree of leaning the body weight forward so that the kick is firm and steady, and the movements are connected, quick and forceful. When pushing the palm, extend the shoulder and the trunk slightly to the right.

Implications for attack and defence: Use the right heel to kick the opponent's knee, and use the right palm to push and hit the opponent's chest.

17. Twist Body, Upper Block and Side Snap Kick

(1) Turn the right tiptoes outward, twist the body and turn the hips to the right. Raise the left heel, slip the foot on the ground half a step forward to the right foot, and bend the left leg slightly. At the same time, change the right palm into fist, bend the elbow and withdraw it to the right side of the waist, fist centre up. Bend the left arm, turn it inward, and move it up for a block obliquely above the head. Look at the left arm. (Fig. 5-26)

(2) Pause a bit after the previous movement (no pause in the duel exercise), shift the body weight to the right leg and stand on it. Raise the left leg and snap it obliquely down to the left, slightly higher than the knee, and instep flat. Look at the left foot. (Fig. 5-27)

Essentials: When turning the body to the right, lower the body weight and move the left foot slightly closer to the right foot to help snap the left leg. The whole exercise should be well-connected and coordinated.

Implications for attack and defence: Use the left fist to parry the opponent's attacking fist, and use the left leg to snap and hit the opponent's abdomen.

18. Press and Hack Palm with Bow Step

Land the left foot forward, and bend the knee to half squat to form the left bow step. Turn the body slightly to the left,

Fig. 5-26   Fig. 5-27

immediately change the right fist into palm, and swing it, arm straight, from behind upward and forward to hack down, thumb up and other fingers forward. At the same time, change the left fist into palm, and press the palm from the front of the body downward to under the right arm, palm facing down (when in duel, continue to press the palm down to the front of the abdomen). Look at the right palm. (Fig. 5-28)

Essentials: Land the left foot before hacking in order to help release force. Hacking and pressing should be completed simultaneously, and coordinated with the power from turning the body.

Implications for attack and defence: Hack with the right palm to strike the opponent's head, and press the left palm to check the fist with which the opponent uses to attack your abdomen.

19. Backward Step, Horse-Riding Step and Parry

Shift the body weight to the right leg, pivot on the ball

of the right foot, and turn the body 90 degrees to the left. After stepping on the ground, move the left foot backward to the left while turning the body and bend the knees to half squat to form the horse-riding step. Change the right palm into fist, bend the elbow, and raise the forearm up to parry to the front of the right chest. Change the left palm into fist and withdraw it to the left side of the waist, fist centre up. Look at the right fist. (Fig. 5-29)

Essentials: Moving the foot backward should be quick. The horse-riding step and the parry should be completed at the same time.

Implications for attack and defence: Use the right forearm to parry the attack from the opponent against your chest.

20. Backward Step, Semi-Horse-Riding Step, Block and Downward Plunge

Shift the body weight to the left leg, pivot on the ball

Fig. 5-28   Fig. 5-29

of the left foot, and turn the body 180 degrees to the right. After stepping on the ground, move the right foot one step to right while turning the body, and bend both legs to the semi-horse-riding step, body weight slightly to the right leg. At the same time, swing the right fist downward, to the right and upward, bend the elbow and place it above the head for a block. Swing the left fist upward to the front of the face, and then turn it inward to plunge it downward to above the left knee, fist face down. Look ahead to the left. (Fig. 5-30)

Essentials: When plunging the left fist downward, pull the forearm slightly backward with force, and in coordination with the upward blocking fist. Relax and lower the shoulders.

Implications for attack and defence: Strike the opponent's head with the back of the right fist, and plunge the left fist downward to ward off the downward punch from the opponent.

21. Bow Step and Push Palm

Turn the body to the left, straighten the right leg, bend the left leg forward to form the left bow step. Change the right fist into palm and push it forward from the right side of the waist, fingers up. Turn the left arm outward, and withdraw the left fist to the left side of the waist, fist centre up. Look ahead. (Fig. 5-31)

Essentials: Push the palm forcefully, extend the right shoulder forward. At the same time, straighten the right leg and turn the hips to help push palm to release force.

Implications for attack and defence: Push the right palm to strike the chest of the opponent.

22. Closing Form

(1) Shift the body weight to the right, turn the body to the right, bend the right leg and straighten the left leg.

Swing the right arm from below to forward, and change the left fist into palm and stretch it to the left side of the body. Keep both arms straight, palms facing left. Look at the right palm. (Fig. 5-32)

(2) Shift the body weight to the left, stand on the left leg, and move the right foot quickly to the left foot. Continue to swing both palms upward, and press them downward to the front of the abdomen, palm facing downward, fingers pointing to each other. Turn the head to the left and look ahead to the left. (Fig. 5-3)

Return to the original position.

Keep both arms down, hands against the outer sides of the thighs, and head front. Look straight ahead. (Fig. 5-1)

Duel

Names of Exercises
1. Starting Form
2. B. Bow Step and Punch
   A. Bow Step, Parry and Spring Fist
3. B. Hook Leg, Bow Step and Press Palm
   A. Raise Knee and Brush Hand
4. A. Forward Step and Snap Kick
   B. Downward Hacking
5. A. Horse-Riding Step and Horizontal Strike
   B. Horse-Riding Step and Outward Parry Palm
6. B. Heel Kick, Bow Step and Push Palm
   A. Change to Jump, Press Palm, Bow Step and Punch
7. B. Twist Body, Upper Block and Side Snap Kick
   A. Backward Step, Side Bow Step and Hammer Strike
8. B. Bow Step, Press and Hack Palm
   A. Bow Step, Block and Uppercut

Fig. 5-30

Fig. 5-31　　　　**Fig. 5-32**

9. A. Forward Step, Bow Step and Push Elbow
   B. Backward Step, Horse-Riding Step and Parry
      Elbow
10. A. Feet Together and Downward Punch
    B. Backward Step, Horse-Riding Step, Block and
       Downward Plunge
11. B. Bow Step and Push Palm
    A. Side Bow Step, Push Elbow and Punch
12. Closing Form

Illustrated Exercises

1. Starting Form

A and B stand with feet together, left shoulder to left shoulder, one step apart. Both look ahead, execute the preparatory form in the single exercise at the same time, and look at each other. (Fig. 5-33)

2. B. Bow Step and Punch (the 11th movement)
A. Bow Step, Parry and Spring Fist (the 1st movement)

(1) B executes the left bow step and thrusts the right fist towards A.

(2) A moves the right leg backward to form the right bow step, and uses the left arm to parry the coming punch from B. (Fig. 5-34) A immediately springs the fist at B's head.

Essentials: B lands his foot in front of A's left foot. A's parry and spring fist should be quick. B stops when A springs his fist at B's face, in order to avoid injuries.

3. B: Hook Leg, Bow Step and Press Palm (the 12th movement)
A: Raise Knee and Brush Hand (the 2nd movement)

(1) B uses the left hand to block and catch A's left fist, and the right hand to support A's left elbow. At the same

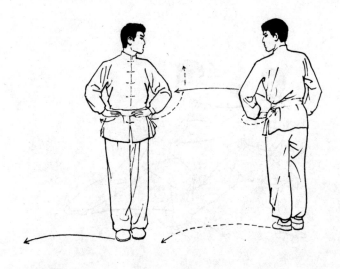

Fig. 5-33

time, B moves the right foot to the inner side of A's left foot, hooks A's left foot backward, executes the bow step and presses palm. (Figs. 5-35, 5-36, 5-37)

(2) A raises the left knee quickly to dodge from B's hook, and at the same time uses the right hand to brush away B's left hand, turns both hands into hooks backward. (Figs. 5-36, 38)

Essentials: A should be quick in raising the knee and brushing the hand, and both movements should be completed at the same time so as to ward off B's movements.

4. A: Forward Step and Snap Kick (the 3rd movement)
B: Downward Hacking (the 13th movement)

(1) A kicks with the right foot at B's abdomen after landing his left foot. (Fig. 5-38)

(2) B immediately withdraws his left foot and hacks down with his left palm to parry A's leg. (Fig. 5-38)

Fig. 5-34

Essentials: A's forward step and kick should be connected and powerful. B can use his palm root or forearm to parry and strike A's right foot or shank, squats down to lower the body weight.

5. A: Horse-Riding Step and Horizontal Strike (the 4th movement)
B: Horse-Riding Step and Outward Parry Palm (the 14th movement)

(1) A lands his right leg to form the bow step, and uses his right fist to strike horizontally at B's head. (Fig. 5-39)

(2) B immediately withdraws his right leg to the horse-riding step, and uses his left palm or forearm to parry A's fist, trunk leaning slightly to the right side to dodge from the attacking fist.

6. B: Heel Kick, Bow Step and Push Palm (the 15th movement)
A: Change to Jump, Press Palm, Bow Step and Punch (the

Fig. 5-35

Fig. 5-36

151

Fig. 5-37

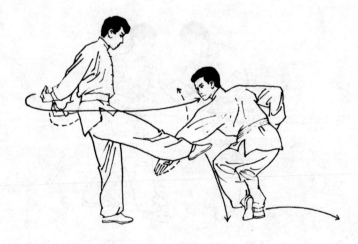

Fig. 5-38

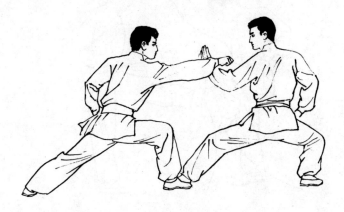

Fig. 5-39

5th movement)

(1) B kick at A's right knee with right foot. (Fig. 5-40)

(2) A immediately withdraws his right fist and raises his right knee backward and upward. (Fig. 5-40)

(3) B lands his right foot and immediately pushes his right palm to A's chest. (Fig. 5-41)

(4) A jumps up a little with his left foot, drops his right foot backward in the air, and lands his left foot in front of B's right foot. A uses his left palm to hold B's right palm, draws B's right palm to the right side, and thrusts his right fist at B. (Figs. 5-41, 5-42)

Essentials: B's kick and push palm should be connected. A should change his foot in good time when jumping up, and appropriately backward in view of B's forward step so as to adjust the distance between them. Only when B pushes his right palm, can A press his palm.

Fig. 5-40

7. B: Twist Body, Upper Block and Side Snap Kick (the 16th movement)
A: Backward Step, Side Bow Step and Hammer Strike (the 6th movement)

(1) B twists his body to the right, uses his left forearm to block A's fist, and immediately uses his left leg to kick at A's abdomen. (Figs. 5-42, 5-43)

(2) A immediately withdraws his left foot to form the left bow step, and uses his right fist back to hammer B's left instep. (Fig. 5-43)

Essentials: A should withdraw his foot quickly and use his right fist back or the outer side of his forearm to hammer B's instep.

8. B: Bow Step, Press and Hack Palm (the 17th movement)
A: Bow Step, Block and Uppercut (the 7th movement)

(1) B lands his foot to form the left bow step, hacks at

Fig. 5-41

Fig. 5-42

Fig. 5-43

A's head with his right palm, and presses his left palm downward to protect the abdomen. (Fig. 5-44)

(2) A forms the right bow step, uses his right hand to block B's right palm. At the same time, uses his left uppercut to strike at B's abdomen. B uses the left palm to check it. (Fig. 5-44)

Essentials: The movements of both sides should be completed at the same time. Pay attention to coordination and cooperation.

9. A: Forward Step, Bow Step and Push Elbow (the 8th movement)
B: Backward Step, Horse-Riding Step and Parry Elbow (the 18th movement)

(1) A moves his foot forward to the left toward B to form the left bow step, and pushes his left elbow toward B's chest. (Fig. 5-45)

(2) B immediately withdraws his left foot to form the

Fig. 5-44

horse-riding step, and uses his right forearm to parry A's elbow. (Fig. 5-45)

Essentials: A moves his foot forward and B withdraws his foot at the same time. A's left foot is in front of B's right foot.

10. A: Feet Together and Downward Punch (the 9th movement)
B: Backward Step, Horse-Riding Step, Block and Downward Plunge (the 19th movement)

(1) A uses his left hand to press off B's right hand, and at the same time moves the feet together, and thrusts his right fist at B's abdomen. (Fig. 5-46)

(2) B immediately withdraws his right foot and uses his left downward plunge to parry off A's fist backward. (Fig. 5-46)

Essentials: A leans his trunk forward when thrusting his fist, and stamps his feet with noises.

Fig. 5-45

Fig. 5-46

Fig. 5-47

11. B: Bow Step and Push Palm (the 20th movement)
A: Side Bow Step, Push Elbow and Punch (the 10th
movement)

(1) B pushes his right palm towards A's chest. (Fig. 5-47)

(2) A withdraws his foot to form the right bow step, and at the same time thrusts his left fist to ward off the attack. (Fig. 5-47)

Essentials: Although the two sides are not in contact in this movement, they look into each other's eyes, both the expression and movements showing that neither side will concede.

12. Closing Form

Both sides execute the closing form in Figs. 5-48,49. They look at each other and return to their original position.

Fig. 5-48

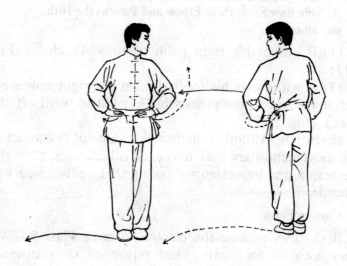

Fig. 5-49

Note: Both sides are permitted not to execute the closing form, but the original movement of the opponent; in other words, A continues to execute the Bow Step and Punch (the 11th movement), while B continues to execute the Bow Step, Parry and Snap Punch (the 1st movement). Continue to do the duel exercises in this order: when A executes the Bow Step and Push Palm (the 20th movement) and B executes the Bow Step, Push Elbow and Punch (the 10th movement), both continue to execute the closing form. It is in this way that the two sides finish all the movements in the duel exercises.

This set of duel exercises is characterized by its flexible foot work, varied content and smooth connections. It has a greater degree of difficulty than the previous set. The quick and continuous completion of the exercises by both sides can demonstrate the method of attack and defence and the characteristic style of the movements true to the actual combat. Beginners should practise them slowly and gradually increase their speed after they become skilled, so as to achieve satisfactory results.

Names of Exercises
1. Starting Form
2. B: Bow Step and Punch
   A: Backward Step and Parry
3. B: Forward Step and Punch
   A: Backward Step and Parry
4. B: Swing Arm and Horizontal Punch
   A: Lower Head to Dodge
5. A: Swing Leg and Kick to Right
   B: Lower Head to Dodge
6. B: Bow Step and Hack palm
   A: Bow Step and Double Palm Block
7. A: Part Palms and Snap Kick

B: Backward Step and Slap Kick
8. A: Land Foot and Punch
   B: Backward Step and Elbow Parry
9. A: Forward Step and Horizontal Sweeping Punch
   B: Backward Step, Twist Body and Upper Block
10. B: Sideways Snap Kick
    A: Dodge and Palm Parry
11. A: Turn Body and Leg Sweep
    B: Raise Knee, Skip Step and Dodge
12. B: Forward Step and Hack Punch
    A: Horse-Riding Step and Elbow Block
13. B: Bow Step and Punch
    A: Horse-Riding Step and Lower Parry
14. B: Bow Step and Double Sweeping Punch
    A: Backward Step and Double Elbow Parry
15. B: Forward Step, Swing Arm and Horizontal Punch
    A: Lower Head to Dodge
16. A: Bow Step and Double Horizontal Punch
    B: Lower Head to Dodge
17. A: Turn Body and Hook Kick
    B: Flash Palm and Raise Knee
18. A and B: Front Slap Kick
19. A and B: Bow Step and Punch
20. Closing Form

Illustrated Exercises

1. Starting Form

(1) A and B stand with feet together in opposite directions, left side to left side, one step apart, and arms down. Both thrust the chest out, keep the abdomen in and look ahead. (Fig. 5-50)

(2) A and B begin the exercise at the same time. Both

raise the arms up from both sides, and when at the head level, press them down in curves in front of the body to the abdomen, palms facing down and fingers pointing to each other and turn the head to the left and look at the opponent. (Fig. 5-51)

Essentials: Keep the movements neat and in unison. When pressing the palms, relax and drop the shoulders, thrust the chest out and withdraw the abdomen.

2. B: Bow Step and Punch
A: Backward Step and Parry

(1) B turns the body to the left, and at the same time moves the left foot forward to form the bow step, changes both palms into fists, thrusts the right fist at A's chest, bends the left elbow and withdraws the fist to the left side of the waist, fist centre up. B looks at the right fist.

(2) A turns the body to the left, immediately withdraws the right foot obliquely backward, turns the right arm outward, bends the elbow and uses the forearm to parry B's right forearm, changes the left palm into fist, bends the elbow, withdraws it to the left side of the waist and look at the right forearm. (Fig. 5-52)

Essentials: B first moves his left foot forward and then thrusts his right fist. A withdraws his foot quickly to help parry with the right arm, turns the trunk slightly to the left and leans it backward. The dodging and parry should be clear.

3. B: Forward Step and Punch
A: Backward Step and Parry

(1) Continue from the previous movement. B moves the right foot forward to form the bow step, thrusts the left fist forward at A's chest, withdraws the right fist to the right side of the waist, elbow bent and looks at the left fist.

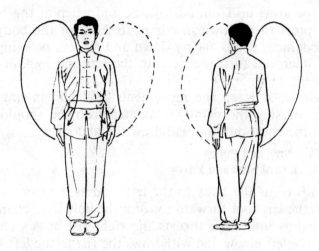

Fig. 5-50

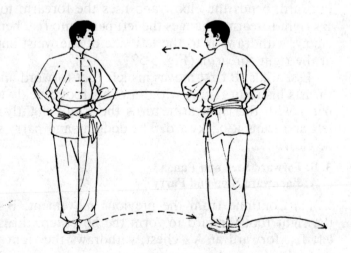

Fig. 5-51

Fig. 5-52

(2) A immediately moves his left foot backward, shifts the body weight backward, and leans the trunk slightly backward. A changes the left fist into palm, turns the arm outward, bends the elbow, parries B's left forearm with the forearm, withdraws the right palm to the right side of the waist, elbow bent and looks at the left forearm. (Fig. 5-53)

Essentials: When B moves his right foot forward, be sure to land it inside of A's right foot. When B moves his foot forward, A immediately moves his left foot backward and shifts his body weight. Both sides should connect their movements with the preceding movements.

4. B: Swing Arm and Horizontal Punch
A: Lower Head to Dodge

(1) B continues to move his left foot forward, tiptoes slightly inward, and, at the same time, swings the right arm forward to A's head and neck from obliquely behind on the

Fig. 5-53

right, fist centre down. B swings the left fist horizontally to
the left side of the body and looks at the right fist.

(2) A moves his right foot backward, ball on the
ground, bends both legs slightly and the trunk forward and
lower the head to dodge when B moves his right fist nearly
to the head. (Fig. 5-54)

(3) B continues to swing the right fist to the left
horizontally, ends the elbow and withdraws it to the chest,
fist centre down. B swings the left arm backward, and
shifts the body weight to the left leg, right heel raised and
looks at the opponent.

(4) A raises the trunk slightly, swings the arms to the
left and looks at the opponent. (Fig. 5-55)

Essentials: When B swings his arm to execute the horizontal punch, keeps the arm straight and applies force to the
fist eye, pressing it low and close to A's body. When A bends
his trunk forward and lowers his head, there should be a

Fig. 5-54

Fig. 5-55

process of lowering his head on B's left side and raising it on the right side. The dodging must be flexible.

5. A: Swing Leg and Kick to Right
B: Lower Head to Dodge

(1) A stands on the left leg, immediately swings the right leg from B's right side, kicks upward towards B's head, and looks at the right foot.

(2) B bends both legs, right foot on the ground, bends the trunk forward, and lowers the head to dodge. (Fig. 5-56)

(3) A continues to swing the right leg to the right, lands the foot obliquely behind the body, and swings the arms naturally to both sides of the body and looks at the opponent.

(4) B raises the trunk upward, swings the arms to the right, bends the left arm and swings it to the chest, palm facing down and right palm facing obliquely up and looks at the opponent. (Fig. 5-57)

Essentials: When A swings his right leg, the movement should be shaped like a Chinese fan, quick and forceful. He should stand firm on the left leg. When B lowers his head to dodge, he is required to do the same as A does in the preceding movement.

6. B: Bow Step and Hack Palm
A: Bow Step and Double Palm Block

(1) B swings the right arm from above forward, hacks at B's head, thumb up and other fingers forward. B clenches the left fist, withdraws it to the left side of the waist, fist centre up, and looks at the right palm.

(2) A lifts both arms above the head, hands crossed, and uses the wrists to block B's hacking palm, right palm below and looks at the hands. (Fig. 5-58)

Essentials: When B swings his arm and hacks with the palm, he should make use of the preceding movement to

Fig. 5-56

Fig. 5-57

Fig. 5-58

release his power, keep the arm straight, and extend the right shoulder. When A blocks, he should begin to cross his hands close to his chest and have the power to push the palms upward.

7. A: Part Palms and Snap Kick
B: Backward Step and Slap Kick

(1) A continues to push the palms upward, part and swing them downward to the two sides of the body, then stands on the left leg, right instep flat, and kicks forward at B's abdomen with the right foot, and looks at the right foot.

(2) B moves his left foot backward, shifts the body weight backward, ball of the right foot on the ground, bends the right arm, withdraws it to the front of the abdomen, and slaps A's right instep, and looks at the hands. (Fig. 5-59)

Essentials: When A kicks, the leg must be first bent and then stretched, and the shank should be neat, quick and

Fig. 5-59

forceful. When B slaps A's right instep with both hands, he should relax both shoulders and bend the arms slightly, his hands having the power to press downward. The slapping should be accurate and loud.

8. A: Land Foot and Punch
B: Backward Step and Elbow Parry

(1) A lands his right foot forward, then immediately thrusts his left fist forward at B's chest, fist eye up, bends the right elbow and withdraws the fist to the right side of the waist, fist centre facing up, and looks at the left fist.

(2) B moves his right foot one step backward, heel slightly raised, changes both palms into fists, bends the right arm, turns it outward, and parries to the outside of A's left forearm. B bends the left elbow and withdraws the fist to the left side of the waist, fist centre facing up, and looks at the opponent. (Fig. 5-60)

Fig. 5-60

Essentials: This movement should immediately follow the previous movement. A should thrust his fist straight and quickly. When B parries, he should react nimbly and make sure to turn the right arm outward.

9. A: Forward Step and Horizontal Sweeping Punch
B: Backward Step, Twist Body and Upper Block

(1) Continue from the preceding movement. A continues to move the left foot forward, and, at the same time, swings the right arm first to lower backward and then to upper forward to execute the curve-shaped sweeping punch at B's head, palm centre facing obliquely down. A bends the left elbow and withdraws the fist to the left side of the waist, and looks at the right fist.

(2) B pivots on the ball of the right foot and stands firmly on the ground, moves the left foot obliquely backward, ball on the ground, bends both legs slightly and

twists the trunk to the right. B then moves the left fist from the chest and face, elbow bent, turns it inward, and places it obliquely above the head for a horizontal block, fist eye facing down. He bends the right elbow and withdraws the fist to the right side of the waist and looks at the left arm. (Fig. 5-61)

Essentials: This movement should immediately follow the preceding movement. When A executes the horizontal sweeping punch, the movement should be quick. He should keep the arm straight, and apply power to the fist eye. When B blocks and parries, the movement should not be too fully extended. The twisting of the body should be compact so as to guard against the opponent's attack.

10. B: Sideways Snap Kick
A: Dodge and Palm Parry

(1) B moves the left foot forward, tiptoes outward,

Fig. 5-61

bends the legs slightly, moves the left arm to the left outside to block away A's right arm, raises the arms naturally on the two sides, and looks at the opponent.

(2) A moves the left foot backward, both legs slightly bent, drops the right arm by the side and looks at the opponent. (Fig. 5-62)

(3) B turns the body to the left, stands on the left leg and immediately swings the right leg to kick forward to the right to A's left shoulder side, instep flat. B then leans the trunk to the left side, raises the left arm obliquely above, drops the right arm naturally and looks at the right foot.

(4) A pivots on the balls of the feet, and turns the body to the left, bends the elbows and withdraws the arms to the front of the chest to meet B's right foot. A then the trunk slightly backward to dodge, and looks at both palms. (Fig. 5-63)

Essentials: B stands firmly on the left leg, and kicks with the shank while raising the right leg. The movement should be quick and nimble with the intention of felling the opponent. A should be nimble in turning the body to dodge from B's attack, and push the palms to slap B's right instep with a loud sound.

11. A: Turn Body and Leg Sweep
B: Raise Knee, Skip Step and Dodge

(1) B turns the body to the right, lands the right foot backward to the right, and with the ball of the left foot on the ground, skips half a step to the right foot, dropping both arms, and looks at the opponent.

(2) A turns the body slightly to the right, moves the left foot forward, tiptoes inward. He shifts the body weight to the left leg, right heel raised, and swings the arms horizontally to the left, and looks at the opponent. (Fig. 5-64)

(3) A bends the left leg quickly to squat, pivots on the ball of the left foot, turns the body to the right, and uses

one falls (as low as the hook level), draw down the opponent.

(2) When the body weight moves backward towards the right leg... move backward and stand upright... the right leg on the ground, not put the weight partly ... side of the back ...

... to face the opponent ...

Push both palms forward ... shoulder-width apart, palms ... should be ... support on ... base and upright ... The purpose of this exercise is ... circle. ... palm forward and ... downward, corresponding and continuous.

13. Kick Forward with Half Palm

4. Horse-Riding Step and Elbow Blow

(1) Retract the left leg forward at waist-level and bend it prior to the ... At the same time, swing the left arm downward, forward and further ... upwards. As stand in front of chest ... push it out. Change the right palm into fist, bend the elbow and swing rearward, the right side of the fist looks toward the left fist.

Fig. 5-62

(2) Retract left leg to right ... continues to swing around ... At the same time ... the body ... and standing upright, swing both ... down the palms forward ... base ... elbow, turn ... and swing rearward above the head with eyes ... towards the right ... fist ... the whole ... turning up. Look at the fist.

Exercise: As backward as forward the eyes should be connected with the preceding movement in a full circle. When exercising with the elbow blow, aim the ... sight ... as the point to attack from the downward ...

Fig. 5-63

the right leg to sweep and hook B's left foot. Look at the opponent.

(4) B shifts the body weight backward, bends the left leg upward and raises it quickly after stepping on the ground, instep flat. Stands on the right leg, skips half a step backward, and raises both palms on both sides of the body, palms facing down. Look at the opponent. (Fig. 5-65)

Essentials: A executes the leg sweep and squats abruptly. The sweeping should be quick, with support on both hands, or with one hand touching the ground lightly. The purpose is to keep balance. B raises the left knee while skipping the step backward, and the movements should be connected and coordinated.

12. B: Forward Step and Hack Punch
A: Horse-Riding Step and Elbow Block

(1) B lands the left foot forward at A's left knee, and bends the knee to the bow step. At the same time, swings the left arm downward, upward and forward, and hacks towards A's head in front of the body, fist eye facing up. Changes the right palm into fist, bends the elbow and withdraws it to the right side of the waist. Look at the left fist.

(2) Before B lands his left foot, A continues to sweep around with the right leg to the right backward, and turns the body 180 degrees to the right, bending both legs to form the horse-riding step. At the same time, bends the left elbow, turns it inward, and blocks horizontally forward above the head, fist eye down. Withdraws the right fist to the right side of the waist, fist centre facing up. Look at the left arm. (Fig. 5-66)

Essentials: A's backward sweep with body turn should be connected with the preceding movement into a full circle. When executing an upper elbow block, lean the trunk slightly to the right to dodge from the downward

Fig. 5-64

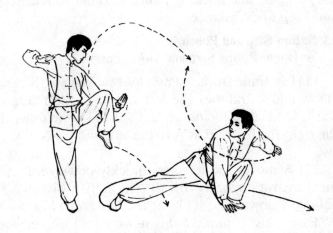

Fig. 5-65

Fig. 5-66

hacking. B should first land the left foot and then execute the swinging and hacking punch in order to release power and keep body balance.

13. B: Bow Step and Punch
A: Horse-Riding Step and Lower Parry

(1) Continue from the previous movement. B bends the elbow and withdraws the left fist to the left side of the waist, fist centre facing up, and, at the same time, thrusts the right fist forward at A to the left, and looks at the right fist.

(2) A moves the left arm quickly downward and uses the forearm to parry off B's right fist, fist eye facing obliquely down, and looks at the left arm. (Fig. 5-67)

Essentials: Complete this movement together with the preceding movement. Both sides keep their stances unchanged, but the attacking and defending movements of

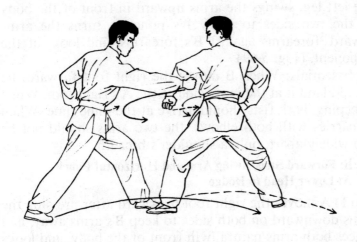

Fig. 5-67

the upper limbs must be quick, simple and neat.

14. B: Bow Step and Double Sweeping Punch
A: Backward Step and Double Elbow Parry

(1) B moves the right foot forward, tiptoes forward and leg slightly bent, bends the arms slightly and swings them backward and obliquely to both sides, both fist eyes up, and looks at the opponent.

(2) A turns the body to the left, moves the left foot backward, tiptoes slightly outward. He swings the arms to the front of the abdomen and crosses them before bending the elbows, right fist outside, and both fist centres facing inward, and looks at the opponent. (Fig. 5-68)

(3) Continue from the above movement. B swings the arms from the two sides in curved shape and sweeps forward above A's ears, fist eye to fist eye, and looks at the opponent.

(4) A bends the right leg slightly forward, straightens the left leg, swings the arms upward in front of the body to the two sides to parry B's punches, turns the arms inward, forearms against B's forearms, and looks at the opponent. (Fig. 5-69)

Essentials: When B moves the right foot forward, he should land it at the inner side of the A's right foot. While sweeping, both fists should arrive at the same time. When A parries with both elbows, the two arms should not be too widely apart, only a shoulder's breadth.

15. B: Forward Step, Swing Arm and Horizontal Punch
A: Lower Head to Dodge

(1) A moves the right foot backward after pressing the arms downward on both sides to keep B's arms away, and places both arms naturally in front of the body, and looks at the opponent.

(2) B moves the left foot forward, leg slightly bent, and swings both arms from below to obliquely backward after they are kept away by A, both fist centres facing down, and looks at the opponent. (Fig. 5-70)

(3) B shifts the body weight forward, straightens the right leg, heel raised, and, at the same time, swings first the left fist and then the right fist horizontally forward and to the left toward A's head or chest and back, and looks at the right fist.

(4) A bends the legs slightly to squat, bends the trunk forward and lowers the head to dodge from B's fists. (Fig. 5-71)

(5) B continues to swing the right arm horizontally to the left, bends the elbow and raises it horizontally in front of the chest, fist centre facing down, and looks ahead.

(6) A raises the trunk up from the left, swings the arms forward to the left, and looks at the opponent. (Fig. 5-72)

Essentials: The same as for the third movement, but B's

Fig. 5-68

Fig. 5-69

Fig. 5-70

Fig. 5-71

Fig. 5-72

swinging of the arms should be immediately connected.

16. A: Bow Step and Double Horizontal Punch
B: Lower Head to Dodge

(1) A quickly swings the arms horizontally forward towards B's head from the left in a curved shape, and looks at the arms.

(2) B lands the right foot firmly, both legs slightly bent, bends the trunk forward, swings the arms downward and lowers the head to dodge. (Fig. 5-73)

(3) A continues to swing the arms to the right, the left arm to the front of the body, and looks at the opponent.

(4) B swings both arms backward, raises the trunk slightly and looks obliquely down. (Fig. 5-74)

Essentials: The same as for the third movement. When A swings the arms to sweep horizontally, he swings both fists forward nearly at the same time.

Fig. 5-73

Fig. 5-74

17. A: Turn Body and Hook Kick
B: Flash Palm and Raise Knee

(1) A pivots on the ball of the left foot, turns the body 180 degrees to the left, stands on the left leg, kicks and hooks with the right leg from the right below B's left foot and to the left forward. He raises the right arm up and moves it backward from forward to form the backhand hook, hook point up, raises the left arm up and flashes the palm obliquely above the head, and looks at the opponent.

(2) B shifts the body weight to the right, stands on the right leg, bends the left leg and raises the knee up, instep flat, raises the right arm obliquely above and the left arm obliquely down, and looks at the opponent. (Fig. 5-75)

Essentials: A first turns the body to the left, then raises the right leg, and flexes the foot and turns the tiptoes to the left when kicking. B should raise the knee lightly, and turn the trunk slightly to the left.

18. A and B: Front Slap Kick

(1) A turns the body to the right and lands the right foot forward. B continues to turn the body to the left and lands the left foot forward. Both shift their body weight forward, heels raised, and raise both arms horizontally forward and backward. Both look ahead. (Fig. 5-76)

(2) B keeps both legs at the same place, swings the left arm from below forward, and the right arm upward, backward, downward and again forward and upward to slap the left palm with the back of the right hand above the head, and looks ahead. (Fig. 5-77)

(3) A shifts the body weight forward, moves the left foot forward, raises the left arm up, and swings the right arm from below forward and upward to slap the left palm with the back of the right hand above the head, and looks ahead. (Fig. 5-77)

Fig. 5-75

Fig. 5-76

Fig. 5-77

(4) A and B Both stand on their left legs, swing the right legs to kick upward, insteps flat, raise the left arms to obliquely above, and move the right palms down to slap the right insteps. Both look at the right palms. (Fig. 5-78)

Essentials: The two partners move neatly and in unison, and slap the palms accurately, clearly and loudly.

19. A and B: Bow Step and Punch

(1) A and B both land their right feet forward, turn their bodies to the left, and shift body weight to between the legs. They drop the right palms and swing them to the lower left, palms facing up, and bend the left palms and withdraw them to above the right forearms, palms facing up, and looks at each other. (Fig. 5-79)

(2) A and B both bend their right legs forward, and straighten the left legs to form the bow step. At the same time, both change the palms into fists, thrust the left fists

Fig. 5-78

Fig. 5-79

forward to the left, and withdraw the right fists horizontally to before the right shoulders, elbows bent, fist centres facing down. They look at each other. (Fig. 5-80)

Essentials: They finish their movements at the same time, and face each other after thrusting the fists. (Fig. 5-80)

20. Closing Form

(1) A and B Both shift the body weight to the left, stand on their left legs, and withdraw right feet to the inner sides of the left feet. At the same time, they raise the arms up from both sides, and press them down in curved shapes to the front of the abdomen when they are at head height, palms facing down, and fingers pointing to each other. Both turn the heads to the left, and look at each other. (See Fig. 5-51)

(2) They keep both arms down and against the outer

Fig. 5-80

Fig. 5-81

sides of the thighs and look straight ahead. (See Fig. 5-50)

(3) A turns the body 180 degrees from the right to join B in the same direction, stands with feet together, and looks straight ahead. (Fig. 5-81)

Essentials: The same as for the Starting Form.

图书在版编目(CIP)数据

长拳拳术提高套路：英文/程慧琨著. —北京：
外文出版社，1995
（中国武术）
ISBN 7-119-01791-8

Ⅰ.长… Ⅱ.程… Ⅲ.长拳—拳术—中国 Ⅳ.G852.12

中国版本图书馆 CIP 数据核字（95）第 09090 号

长拳拳术提高套路

程慧琨

*

©外文出版社
外文出版社出版
（中国北京百万庄路 24 号）
邮政编码 100037
北京外文印刷厂印刷
中国国际图书贸易总公司发行
（中国北京车公庄西路 35 号）
北京邮政信箱第 399 号　邮政编码 100044
1996 年（大 32 开）第 1 版
（英）
ISBN 7-119-01791-8 /G·89(外)
01660
7-E-3044P